# CASTING A SHADOW

Mary and Leigh Block Museum of Art, Northwestern University

Northwestern University Press

# CASTING A SHADOW

## CREATING THE ALFRED HITCHCOCK FILM

*Edited by*

WILL SCHMENNER and CORINNE GRANOF

*Exhibition curated by*

WILL SCHMENNER

*Contributions by*

DAVID ALAN ROBERTSON,

WILL SCHMENNER, SCOTT CURTIS,

TOM GUNNING, BILL KROHN, JAN OLSSON

*Casting a Shadow: Creating the Alfred Hitchcock Film* is published in conjunction with a traveling exhibition organized by the Mary and Leigh Block Museum of Art, Northwestern University.

MARY AND LEIGH BLOCK MUSEUM OF ART
Northwestern University
Evanston, Illinois
September 29–December 9, 2007

ACADEMY OF MOTION PICTURE ARTS
AND SCIENCES
Beverly Hills, California
January 18–April 20, 2008

This exhibition and related programs were made possible with the suppport of the Hitchcock Foundation, Dr. James Pick and Dr. Rosalyn Laudati, the Louis Family Foundation, the Myers Foundation, the Alice Kaplan Institute for the Humanities, Northwestern University, American Airlines, and the Illinois Arts Council, a state agency.

Published by the Mary and Leigh Block Museum of Art and Northwestern University Press, Evanston, Illinois 60208.

Designed by Diane Jaroch Design
Copyedited by Kingsley Day
Printed in Canada by Friesens Corporation
Color separations by Prographics

In the face of considerable challenges in identifying copyright holders of film production materials, the publishers have made every reasonable effort to locate those copyright holders and obtain permission to use materials presented in this publication. Copyright holders are identified, where possible, in the illustration and plate captions.

*Published in honor of Lawrence B. Dumas and his many years of service and leadership at Northwestern University.*

LIBRARY OF CONGRESS CATALOGING-IN-PUBLICATION DATA

Casting a shadow : creating the Alfred Hitchcock film / curated by Will Schmenner; edited by Corinne Granof and Will Schmenner; contributions by David Alan Robertson ... [et al.].

p. cm.

Published in conjunction with an exhibition organized by the Mary and Leigh Block Museum of Art, Northwestern University and held at the Mary and Leigh Block Museum of Art Sept. 29–Dec. 9, 2007 and the Academy of Motion Picture Arts and Sciences, Beverly Hills, Calif. Jan. 18–Apr. 20, 2008.

Includes bibliographical references and index.
ISBN-13: 978-0-8101-2447-9 (pbk. : alk. paper)
ISBN-10: 0-8101-2447-5 (pbk. : alk. paper)
1. Hitchcock, Alfred, 1899–1980—Criticism and interpretation. 2. Hitchcock, Alfred, 1899–1980—Exhibitions. 3. Motion pictures—Production and direction—Exhibitions. 4. Art and motion pictures—Exhibitions. I. Schmenner, Will. II. Granof, Corinne. III. Robertson, David Alan. IV. Mary and Leigh Block Museum of Art. V. Academy of Motion Picture Arts and Sciences.
PN1998.3.H58C37 2007
791.430233092—dc22

2007029080

# Contents

## Acknowledgments

It is appropriate that a book about the role of collaboration in making movies is itself a collaborative effort. David Alan Robertson, the Ellen Philips Katz Director of the Mary and Leigh Block Museum of Art, and I first discussed film production within the larger context of artistic collaboration and historical collaborative processes. His desire to see a Block Museum exhibition explore the place of motion pictures in the fine arts museum made this project possible.

The Margaret Herrick Library made many invaluable contributions to this project. The Library's director, Linda Mehr, embraced the idea of the exhibition in its earliest stages of conception. I am deeply grateful for her willingness to loan the bulk of the works included in the exhibition. Also at the Herrick Library, Barbara Hall generously shared her profound knowledge of the collections, her time, and her expertise. Anne Coco seamlessly mixed insights with encouragement, while Jenny Romero's resourcefulness and organizational ability was crucial to the success of this project. Ellen Harrington's interest and counsel continue to be a great help. Faye Thompson's knowledge of the photograph archive enlivened the book.

Also in Los Angeles and vicinity, Eric Weismann generously shared his legal expertise, opening many doors necessary to obtain copyright for the works of art in the exhibition and publication. I deeply appreciate the generous support and encouragement provided by Dr. James Pick and Dr. Rosalyn Laudati. I am also grateful to Leland Faust, Patricia Hitchcock O'Connell, and the Hitchcock Foundation for supporting the project. The kind assistance of Cindy Chang and Roni Lubliner at Universal Studios, Andy Bandit and Schawn Belston at Twentieth Century Fox, Julie Heath and Darlene Grodske at Warner Bros., and Larry McAllister at Paramount Pictures enabled the exhibition and publication to move forward.

In London, Amanda Nevill, director of the British Film Institute, encouraged me to proceed with my thesis, while Michael Caldwell and Carolyne Bevan kindly shared the BFI's extensive archives. Janet Moat oversaw loans critical to telling the story presented in this publication and the exhibition.

Northwestern University Press partnered with the Block Museum to make the publication possible. For that, I thank Henry Carrigan Jr., Parneshia Jones, Sara Hoerdeman, and especially Donna Shear.

Diane Jaroch, the book's devoted designer, has beautifully framed the contributors' ideas. I cannot thank her enough for her hard work and attention to detail.

The student volunteers at Block Cinema have stepped up as I have had to step away from some of my day-to-day responsibilities to work on this project. I'm grateful to them all, especially Kyle Smith, Arturo Menchaca, and Jason Klorfein. Block Graduate Fellow Margaret O'Neill spent many hours comparing drawings and sketches to film clips, analysis that has been vital to the project. Andy Garland, Meredith Ward, and Shelia Burt did important research for the exhibition when it was little more than an idea. Lindsay Amini, Kevin Brown, Ashley Carpenter, Kingsley Day, and Jamie Dobie have worked tirelessly to prepare the publication and exhibition. Beyond Northwestern University, Nicholas Day helped with insightful editing. Ryan Hubbard and David Mulcahey kindly participated in copyediting. My parents Roger and Barbara Schmenner encouraged and inspired me throughout.

I am indebted to the entire staff of the Block Museum for their counsel and support. My early conversations with Dan Silverstein were critical for their insight. Debora Wood, senior curator, and Kristina Bottomley, registrar, generously helped in numerous ways from sharing crucial advice to catching important details. Amy Brandolino's enthusiasm and wisdom helped shape the Hitchcock programming. Burke Patten employed considerable talent to share the story with the press and our audiences. Nicole Druckman and Helen Hilken worked hard to secure financial support for the project. James Foster, Paul Dougherty, and Aaron Chatman oversee Museum security during this and all exhibitions. I am grateful to Mary Hirsh and Carole Towns for constant administrative support. I wish to thank my co-editor, Corinne Granof, for sharing her extraordinary talents to ensure the success of the publication.

Finally, thanks go out to Scott Curtis, Tom Gunning, Bill Krohn, and Jan Olsson for contributing their valuable perspectives on Alfred Hitchcock in the pages that follow.

WILL SCHMENNER

To many Alfred Hitchcock (1899–1980) embodies the idea of the film director as artist. Indeed, this was a persona he carefully nurtured throughout his career, relying heavily upon well-established tropes for artistic identity and genius long codified in Western culture. Screenwriter Larry Gross characterizes this aspect of Hitchcock's persona and his attitude toward the processes and people required to materialize his film ideas:

Hitchcock announces that nothing about the physical fact of filmmaking interests him. All the essential creative work has been wrapped up before he comes to the set. Making the film is a tedious, nearly impertinent necessity, grafted on to the authentic creative work that has already been done.[1]

To enforce this image of the director as conceptual artist, Hitchcock talked about the importance of envisioning his films before the cameras began to roll. When interviewed by the French film director François Truffaut in 1962, Hitchcock boasted," I never look at a script while I'm shooting. I know the whole film by heart."[2]

In interviews throughout his career, Hitchcock isolated and elevated the film director above other actors and processes involved in film production. In an article written for the *London Evening News* early in his career in 1927, he coined the term "one-man pictures," writing:

Film directors live with their pictures while they are being made. They are babies just as much as an author's novel is the offspring of his imagination. And that seems to make it all the more certain that when moving pictures are really artistic they will be created entirely by one man.[3]

Hitchcock's somewhat mixed metaphors here suggest images of the film director as father, nurturer, author, and sole inventive genius, typologies that served to advance his career, his movies, and, in a more general sense, the status of the film director as well as the medium of film itself. In some ways, since Hitchcock's time, these ideas have

served to support the argument for motion pictures as a fine art. The founding tenet framing the argument for the director as artist remains that he or she controls the central creative aspects of a film's production.

Intimately related to—and in many ways inseparable from—this carefully crafted, if reductive, artist identity is Hitchcock's extensive use of drawings, notably storyboards, to envisage entire film sequences. These comic-strip-like drawings—rooted in Hitchcock's educational background in drafting and design—were used extensively in his film productions to frame scenes and delineate action. They were additionally used by his publicists to prove his prescient vision and artistic control. This is regardless of the fact that these are rarely monographic and were actually done by specialist artists in the employ of the studio. The lengths to which he and his promoters went to perpetuate this image of director as film designer are revealed in an excerpt from a letter (page 24)—first published by Bill Krohn—that was written by Hitchcock's publicist, Rick Ingersoll, and refers to the then soon-to-be-released film *North by Northwest*:

I'm sending about 13 stills from which I would like Mr. Hitchcock to make the sketches I discussed with him before he left for Europe. As a reminder, they are for Coronet magazine—and theoretically sketches he made before the scenes were filmed. This is for a layout in which his sketches and the resultant scenes would be compared, to show how he maps out every detail of his productions before the scenes are photographed.[4]

Several storyboards drawn after the filming are clearly of the actor Cary Grant. The fabrication of these drawings should have been evident, since storyboards are normally drawn before casting.

Contrary to the facts of his film work and the highly complex, technologically anchored, and collaborative nature of the medium, Hitchcock wove artist-images of the film director for the same public consumption for which his films themselves were conceived. To proclaim this status, he drew in eccentric and often charming ways upon a well-established art-historical construction—the artist as lone genius.

Hitchcock's archetype—with its emphasis on creative genius over collaboration, conceptualization over fluidity of design—is an old one in Western art. It emerged at the beginning of the Renaissance as visual artists—most notably Michelangelo Buonarroti and Albrecht Dürer—struggled to disassociate themselves from guilds and their workshop satellites and identify with the higher artistic realms long afforded to the more contemplative art forms of musical composition and literature. That is, they fervently wished to establish parity for visual artists with artists who were not primarily identified as working with their hands. These Renaissance visual artists were thus not only challenging the artistic glories of the ancient past, but also competing with artists working in other media for a status afforded to intellectuals and gentlemen and not craftsmen. By their dazzling achievements and their emphasis on the primacy of originality of thought—something for which the Italians variously applied the word *invenzione*—over artisanship, these artists and their early biographers such as Giorgio Vasari and Ascanio Condivi succeeded in one generation to permanently elevate the status of painters, sculptors, and architects in Western culture from craftsmen to artists.

To this day the Renaissance epitomizes the ideals of artistic genius and commanding individuality, personified by such titans as Leonardo da Vinci, Raphael, Michelangelo, and Dürer. Michelangelo's creative genius, to note one famous instance, resulted in his receiving in his lifetime the appellation "Il Divino." He was thus lauded because his visual worlds were so powerful in capturing not just the material consequence but also the essence of God's creative power. Another example of this sense of elevated status for the artist is Dürer's 1492 self-portrait, done after an eye-opening trans-Alpine trip. The artist portrays himself vested as a Venetian gentleman complete with elegant gloves, that is to say, as one who fundamentally works by his wit and only incidentally by his hands. Self-portraiture remains a powerful statement of self-awareness

and self-respect, and in Dürer's time, a demonstration of creativity beyond artworks made on commission, the lifeblood of workshops. While Dürer created a sequence of independent self-portraits throughout his life, Raphael often included images of himself among onlookers standing near the margins of his religious and allegorical paintings. Such "cameo" appearances served both as a visual signature for the artist and as a pronouncement of the painter's place in his compositions, as pious witness and as intermediary between inspiring imagery and the viewer. In this light it is noteworthy that the practice of artists signing their works was generally unheard of before the Renaissance, but became commonplace in the visual arts thereafter. In short, visual artists became inseparably identified with invention, and their identities and unique creative geniuses remain the core of the monographic approach to the history of art that in fact originated during the Renaissance with Vasari's *Lives of the Most Eminent Painters, Sculptors, and Architects* (1550).

In the early 1980s, coinciding with a revival of collaborative art practices—particularly the joining of monumental sculpture, painting, and mosaic programs with public building and other large "percent for art" projects—art historians advanced contextual approaches to the past. They particularly showed an interest in the relationship between art commissions and their original locations, their programmatic underpinnings and source materials, and the complex collaborative workshop practices that brought them into being. By means of this expanded methodology, a counterview to the artist as lone genius was explored.

Among the eye-opening scholarly writings in this light was William E. Wallace's 1987 *Gazette des Beaux-Arts* article "Michelangelo's Assistants on the Sistine Chapel."[5] Wallace's article coincided with and was influenced by a large-scale cleaning of the Sistine frescoes and the opportunity to view the work up close from the conservators' scaffolding. While both Vasari and Michelangelo's biographer Condivi mention Michelangelo's assistants in their biographies of the artist, they were, for the most part, dismissive of their roles and generally restrict these individuals to activities such as grinding and mixing colors for the master. Wallace notes, to the contrary, that at the time of the Sistine commission in 1508, Michelangelo had had little experience in fresco painting. Among thirteen Florentine assistants identified by Wallace were several hired for these very skills by Michelangelo from the workshop of his former master, the painter Domenico Ghirlandaio. Wallace also translated records suggesting that these individuals continued to work on the ceiling, even at times when the master was known to be away from the project.[6] Based on records and a close study of the various hands present in the painting itself, Wallace suggested that these assistants not only built scaffolding, mixed colors, and transferred large-scale drawings, called cartoons, to the ceiling surface, but also painted entire passages such as architectural details, putti, and medallions. This revelation stands in sharp contrast to the image of Michelangelo in art-historical monographs, or for that matter as portrayed by Charlton Heston in the film *The Agony and the Ecstasy* (1965) as a lone, indefatigable megalomaniac. Wallace's iconoclastic approach, along with the long-suggested role of at least one Vatican scholar, Marco Vigerio, in advising Michelangelo on the frescoes' theological programs, considerably broadened the story of one of the great monuments of Western art and suggested not only a genius for invention, but also, on some level, a capacity for dynamic collaboration with Michelangelo.

In Hitchcock's time the artist as lone genius was a cultural commonplace further refined by a growing characterization from the late 19th century onward of artists as isolated from society, eccentric, and bohemian. With a keen sense of the power of publicity, Hitchcock created a memorable public facade for himself as artist and thus fulfilled his desire to place the director at the vortex of the creative aspects of film. His overt and caricature-like embrace of several art-historical tropes for himself and for the popular medium of film resounds in his words—as referenced above—and manifests itself through his notable appearances in the press, in film, and eventually on television. Ranging from contractual requirements that his name be placed in lettering of specific size on posters for his films to his much anticipated, often funny, and highly mem-

orable film cameos (page 72), Hitchcock pronounced his omnipresence in films under his direction and associated himself and the new art form with signature and visual conceits associated for centuries with fine artists. He even required, at times, that his famous profile or entire rotund figure be included on film posters, where he, like artists before him, stood in the margins and served as interlocutor between the artwork's message and its viewers.

Regardless of this posturing, Hitchcock, like the great masters before him, obviously stood at the head of a large and creative workshop of artists, artisans, and technicians. Actual documents, cited in this publication and included in the accompanying exhibition, tell a different story than Hitchcock's carefully crafted public persona allowed. They reveal an even more intriguing and remarkable story of collaboration and delicate creative processes that involved many people making decisions in a layered, multistep process. Indeed, Hitchcock's working methods were flexible—allowing other people to come up with ideas critical to the picture and making room for changes to the movie while he was on the set. In doing this, he engaged the best talents in the field, Robert Boyle and Henry Bumstead for production design, Academy Award-winning costume designer Edith Head, and even artist Salvador Dali to inspire an important dream sequence in the film *Spellbound* (1945), to name but a few. From this perspective, Hitchcock emerges as a man orchestrating, indeed directing—rather than as a medium channeling—his vision through his workshop. It is an image that is at once more believable and more impressive than the myth.

Revealing of Hitchcock's collaborative method was his initial approach to creating a film of Daphne du Maurier's 1952 novella *The Birds*. After reading the book, Hitchcock's first action was to turn it over to production designer Robert Boyle to read and then for Boyle to draw images of his choosing, based upon the narrative (plate 1). The purpose of these drawings was to help Hitchcock imagine the novel's cinematic possibilities before committing to the project. Indeed, Hitchcock's profuse use of drawing is comparable to the historical employment of that direct medium to design frescoes, panel paintings, and prints in the art of the past. While appreciated since the time of Vasari as works of art in and of themselves, the vast majority of surviving Old Master drawings are in fact process drawings. Their original purpose was to serve as designs for the creation of artworks in other media. Exhibitions of such drawings from the past are commonplace in museums: Hitchcock's process drawings included in the accompanying exhibition, while not appreciated by most today as fine art, nonetheless served the very same studio and workshop functions.

Although his publicity machine would often point to the drawings (particularly the storyboard drawings) as proof of Hitchcock's singular control of films made under his direction, the original documents—noteworthy for the multiple hands involved in their creation—strongly suggest a different reality. Their often reworked states and obvious pentimenti show an evolving approach to framing scenes and camera angles. They reveal a vibrant dialogue within Hitchcock's circle, and the notations on several provide evidence that this was done during filming.

While Hitchcock's self-promotion capitalized upon commonplace attitudes embedded in popular imagination toward art making and artists, his actual workshop practices more accurately associate his creative genius with art practices. The story of his collaborative skills, while more complex and clearly less exciting to stir popular notions of the art of filmmaking, nonetheless reveal an equally impressive genius. It is genius to create a unified work of art and corpus of films that engaged large numbers of talented individuals in the process.

DAVID ALAN ROBERTSON
*The Ellen Philips Katz Director*

# CASTING A SHADOW

*Left to right:* Production designer Henry Bumstead, unit production manager C. O. "Doc" Erickson, director Alfred Hitchcock, and associate producer Herbert Coleman discuss a production design drawing on the set of *The Man Who Knew Too Much* (1956). Still courtesy of the Academy of Motion Picture Arts and Sciences. Rights courtesy of Universal Studios Licensing LLLP.

# Creating the Alfred Hitchcock Film: An Introduction

WILL SCHMENNER

In 1954 the cultural critic and intellectual Robert Warshow wrote:

[T]here is art in the movies, and there is an "art" cinema. Many of the products of "art" cinema well deserve all the praise they have received. And yet, I think, one cannot long frequent the "art" cinema or read much of the criticism which upholds it without a sense of incompleteness and even of irrelevance. Really the movies are not quite that "legitimate"—they are still the bastard child of art, and if in the end they must be made legitimate, it will be a changed household of art which receives them.[1]

Over fifty years later there is still something about movies in the fine arts museum that raises eyebrows. It is a problem of exhibition: movies aren't meant for clean, bright museum walls. It is a problem of technology and medium: a movie is not a unique object and cannot be appreciated without the technology to project it. And it is a problem of authorship: movies do not conform to our ideas of how art should be created.

It is the last of these problems that is the most nebulous and potentially rewarding. Indeed, the exhibition and this catalogue, although specifically about Alfred Hitchcock, focus more generally on the issue of how movies are created. At the heart of the problem is a paradox: movies are made by scores, even hundreds of people, and movies are the creation of the director. How can this be?

To pose the question another way, we talk about movies as if they belonged to a director, for instance, Alfred Hitchcock's *The Birds* (1963). To a certain extent *The Birds* is Alfred Hitchcock's. But is it Alfred Hitchcock's in the same way that *Ulysses* is James Joyce's? In the same way *Mona Lisa* is Leonardo da Vinci's? Perhaps unlike most of literature and many types of painting, feature film production has always been a collaborative venture. The very nature of feature film production requires it to be. Yet much of the politics of the Hollywood studio system, the vagaries of marketing, the organization of film programming in museums and cinematheques, and even film criticism itself have often opted to ignore film's collaborative nature in an effort to legitimize film as art. When the collective creativity within movies is pushed aside, one can argue that movies are art because directors are artists. However, such a statement is only part of the truth. The goal of this exhibition and catalogue is to demonstrate that collaboration and artistic legitimacy are not mutually exclusive. The relatively new medium of film (compared with the other arts, film is still just a toddler) demands a rethinking of authorship.

The myths surrounding Alfred Hitchcock and his own ambiguous position in regards to authorship, coupled with the production designs, sketches, storyboards, and other collaborative documents from his productions, make him and his work an ideal focus for an exhibition concerned with authorship and how movies are created. After briefly examining the idea of authorship in film, this essay will turn its attention to Hitchcock's own words and drawings from his productions, as well as introduce the other essays and the plate section.

Motion pictures first prominently entered the fine arts museum in 1935 when the director of the Museum of Modern Art, Alfred H. Barr Jr., hired Iris Barry to start the museum's Film Library. Barry needed a group of quality films that would implicitly strengthen the claim that film belonged in the fine arts museum; in other words, she needed a canon. In fact, at the time there was no video, no television, and few repertory cinemas, and only the most recent films were available for viewing. More than anyone's, Barry's programming and preservation efforts helped create a film canon. Interestingly, her evolving film canon was authorless. Barry and others were still primarily arguing for the categorical uniqueness of movies. For motion pictures to be considered an art form, they had to be their own new and separate art. As intellectuals like Vachel Lindsay and Hugo Münsterberg had argued since the 1910s, movies were art because they were not theater, music, painting, or photography. Within this context part of what made movies unique was that they did not have authors in the typical sense of the word. Indeed, resolving the sticky question of authorship in film was not seen as a priority.

Eighty-five years ago, movies had yet to make their foray into the fine arts museum. Iris Barry would soon be a founding member of the London Film Society. And producer Michael Balcon first met Hitchcock at Islington Studios. Balcon, as much as Barry, wished to improve film's reputation—it was generally seen as rather classless, cheap entertainment. Balcon intrinsically understood the motion picture business needed directors who could raise people's expectations of what movies could be. His money was on Hitchcock, who had the potential to impress with both his carefully controlled image and his precisely constructed movies. Working for Gaumont-British and later Ealing Films, Balcon not only gave Hitchcock his first credited job as a director, he also helped cultivate Hitchcock's reputation as the master of suspense. The exhibition includes two pages of notes from Michael Balcon. There he reviews the projects he is working on and asks himself if the script for *The 39 Steps* (1935) "is any good for a director other than A.J.H."[2] Balcon was a man intimately acquainted with the collaborative work it took to make a movie. Yet he also understood that *The 39 Steps* was likely to be a movie that Hitchcock could make better than anyone else. As his notes reveal, he realized, perhaps around the same time as Hitchcock, that there could be such a thing as a Hitchcock picture, and, indeed, he nurtured its development.

Contrary to our usual notions of film authorship, the development of the Hitchcock film does not mean Hitchcock controlled all the aspects of production or dominated his early films. An early contract from *The Skin Game* (1931), a motion picture Hitchcock made for John Maxwell of British International Pictures, bound Hitchcock to the written scenario, prohibiting him from changing it during filming.[3] Although in the case of *The Skin Game* Hitchcock may have had an advantage over other directors similarly obliged—*The Skin Game* was written by Alma Reville, a well-known scenario writer and film editor and also Hitchcock's wife—he still was in a position where carefully planning his production and collaborating with his writer would afford him the best chance to make a quality movie. Hitchcock planned, perhaps because he was compelled by artistic inspiration, but also out of necessity. Because he was contractually obliged to film the scenario, the only means he had for controlling the quality of the film was meticulous preparation. And it is here at the intersection of creating and planning that Hitchcock's greatness is too often unexamined—it is that greatness that Balcon may very well have seen in

Director Alfred Hitchcock on
the set of *The Birds* (1963). Still
courtesy of the Academy of
Motion Picture Arts and Sciences.
Rights courtesy of Universal
Studios Licensing LLLP.

Director Alfred Hitchcock and cinematographer Robert Burks planning a shot on the set of *The Trouble with Harry* (1955). Still courtesy of the Academy of Motion Picture Arts and Sciences. Rights courtesy of Universal Studios Licensing LLLP.

Hitchcock 85 years ago. It may be unexamined in part because it is still problematic. The process raises many questions and goes to the core of what it means to direct a film.

The writers from *Cahiers du cinéma* in the 1950s approached the problem of authorship from a different perspective. From their position as critics and writers, the director was both the person most responsible for a film and the only person among the various department heads whose contributions to the film were unidentified. The actors have their performances. The screenwriter has his or her script. The cinematographer has the film itself. But what is the director's? *Cahiers* writers wished to establish a categorical way of judging directorial efforts, and they wanted to bring motion pictures into the pantheon of arts.

Although the precise articulation of *la politique des auteurs* depended upon which critic was writing, it was typically an argument that positioned the director as a movie's creator and artist. Part of *la politique des auteurs* was an effort to uncover the signature of the director within the abundance of information a film provides. The writers at *Cahiers du cinéma* maintained that "mise-en-scène" was where one would primarily find the director's voice. Mise-en-scène means, more or less, that which is placed in the scene, and it can include such facets of directing as blocking, aspects of set design, camera techniques, and color motifs. They kept the category deliberately vague, perhaps because directors, depending on their power and abilities, had control over varying aspects of a production. *La politique des auteurs* was, at its heart, a way of seeing a film—one that allowed someone with no prior knowledge of how a particular film was made to understand a director's contribution to a given film. In a sense, it was a way of understanding movies, which encouraged dissecting how they were made. This approach opened up a new world of film analysis.[4]

Hitchcock became a perennial illustration of the *Cahiers* argument with his tendency to make movies that were variations on a given theme (for instance, the innocent man wrongly accused), his well-known collaborations with his writers, and

his own arguments for the importance of the director. If only for a moment, *la politique des auteurs* was primarily about finding the director's voice in a movie. For example, although director Nicholas Ray did not write or produce many of his own films, his movies had his touch. Through mise-en-scène he made a vital aspect of the movie his own. However, *la politique des auteurs* quickly, if not immediately, expanded from an advocacy for the director's essential shaping and leading influence upon a film into an argument for the director as author and sole artist. Iris Barry had begun the creation of the canon, and *Cahiers* proceeded to enumerate the authors. Perhaps *Cahiers'* list of authors was an inevitable step in the efforts to legitimize movies. However, it placed these two arguments for film as art at odds with one another. Barry and others had argued motion pictures were a unique art form, while the more zealous writers at *Cahiers* had argued for directors as auteurs, where an auteur was interchangeable with an author or an artist.[5]

Hitchcock's own self-promotion foreshadowed his later auteur status. Long before *Cahiers* published its first article on *la politique des auteurs*, Hitchcock discussed his desire to make one-man pictures. On November 16, 1927, an article by Hitchcock appeared in the *London Evening News* titled "Films We Could Make." In it he claimed, "Film directors live with their pictures while they are being made. They are their babies just as much as an author's novel is the offspring of his imagination. And that seems to make it all the more certain that when moving pictures are really artistic they will be created entirely by one man."[6] It was a  bold claim that some of his later writing would contradict.

It may be nearly impossible to determine precisely when the director became the artist behind the film.[7] But after a certain moment, it was no longer revolutionary to argue for a way of seeing movies that emphasized the director's contributions. Indeed, even Hitchcock's strident argument for one-man pictures no longer seemed overly simplistic. Today, for example, we are more likely to understand *la politique des auteurs* as an argument for one-man pictures than as an insight into how movies are made. Hitchcock's mythology, however manufactured, has become the textbook example of an auteur, despite the evidence of how he actually worked. In fact, the word auteur is used not to suggest how movies are an art form but as an expression of a director's power, influence, and almost fervent independence (coupled with a hunger for credit) regardless of the quality of the work. For example, it is employed to describe someone who writes, produces, and directs his movies, not in collaboration but by himself.

Although Hitchcock eventually produced his own movies and often oversaw the writing of his films, it would be a mistake to see Hitchcock in this light. To understand how Hitchcock worked we must separate the self-promoter from the filmmaker. Hitchcock was attuned to the public's need for a direct relationship between artist and art object, providing that connection from his early argument for one-man pictures to his later claim that he envisioned his movies entirely in his mind before they went into production. Inasmuch as his greatness seemed apparent (both in his movies and in his persona), and inasmuch as the public perceived a satisfyingly direct relationship between artist and art object, many accepted what on the face of it was a rather ridiculous claim: that Hitchcock made his movies essentially by himself. For many the claim is imbued with a mythic quality—as if Hitchcock's movies sprung from his head fully formed, like Athena from Zeus. Hitchcock even reinforced that interpretation with the occasional claim to be more of a motion picture shaman than a director. Hitchcock knew that public personas do not need to be consistent in order to be effective. A certain amount of contradiction creates mystery and, ironically, a more convincing illusion of reality. Hitchcock reveled from time to time in inflammatory comments, and about not just his ability to visualize, but, for instance, dealing with actors—"they should be treated like cattle." He did, however, occasionally speak with honesty about his working methods.[8]

Much of his writing from the late 1930s reads like a personal philosophy on filmmaking. In the article "Life Among the Stars," he began by enumerating all of the crew and comparing them to an army: "disciplined, departmentalized, and efficient." Later on in that same series of articles he wrote about how he makes his films: "We want to find a story. We meet and talk. We read reviews—we have no time to read the whole books. We pore over notices of plays."[9] The "we" that Hitchcock invoked likely included his key collaborators. Hitchcock's desire for meaningful collaboration had not abated over 20 years later when Hitchcock was working on *The Birds* with screenwriter Evan Hunter. After receiving an early draft of the script from Hunter, he shared it with his collaborators and synthesized their comments with his in the response to Hunter:

The script has also been read by a number of other people, mostly the technicians who are working on the picture, such as art director, production personnel, etc. probably not more than 8 or 9 people in all.

With the comments I have, I'm also going to include their observations. Naturally, of course, where someone might have made some comment which I didn't agree with I am, as Sam Goldwyn would say, "including them out."

The first general impression is that the script is way too long. This, of course, I know you are already aware of. However the consensus seems to indicate that it is the front part of the script that needs some drastic pruning. I will suggest some ideas to you later on in this letter.

Now the next prevalent comment I have heard is that both the girl and the young man seem insufficiently characterized. In endeavoring to analyze this criticism I have gathered the impression "there doesn't seem to be any particular feature about the young man himself to warrant the girl going to all the trouble she does in delivering a couple of love birds."[10]

Hitchcock is more interested in the consensus than in identifying his thoughts or those of any individual collaborator. In the letter to Hunter he goes on to expand upon the critique with a specific story explaining the danger of "'no-scene' scenes." Although he claims the story as his, he has no desire to reveal where his opinions end and where the thoughts of his department heads begin. There is every reason to believe that when Hitchcock wrote that the "most valuable thing in creating a film is criticism at the time," he meant it, both for himself and for his collaborators. Indeed, he created an environment that fostered constructive criticism.[11]

The boundaries of that critical yet collaborative environment was the general idea of the Alfred Hitchcock film. The Alfred Hitchcock film was specific enough that it was Hitchcock's, yet broad enough that other people could contribute to it. And people certainly did contribute—recommending books, stories, and plays that had that certain Hitchcock feel.[12]

The contributions he sought most eagerly were with very talented people and were profoundly collaborative. The drawings, sketches, storyboards, correspondences, and documents from his productions reveal a process that puts Hitchcock in the center of a mess of such collaborations. He is more workman than shaman, and with the consistent collaboration of his department heads, he is visualizing and revisualizing his films, synthesizing disparate thoughts, and incorporating suggestions into the project's original idea.

The plates in the final section of this catalogue are evidence that Hitchcock was not the only one envisioning the movie. The writers, the production designers, the costume designers, the cinematographers all created objects that responded to Hitchcock's suggestions and advanced a more detailed visualization of the movie. Parsing such an organic process for credit becomes at a point counterproductive. Our search for individual authorship within this collective process risks misunderstanding and devaluing what it means to produce a collectively created vision. What is valuable about dissecting how the Alfred Hitchcock film was made is not, for example, the ability to ascertain that such-and-such suggestion was made by the cinematographer, but rather to understand that the process of creating a movie is highly collaborative in a manner that is unique to

motion pictures. The better we understand the creative process behind motion pictures, the better we can understand cinema's place within our culture and within the fine arts museum. Here is Hitchcock's earthiest description of the film-making process:

We went into a huddle and slowly from discussions, arguments, random suggestions, casual, desultory talk, and furious intellectual quarrels as to what such and such a character in such and such a situation would or would not do, the scenario began to take shape.

The difficulty of writing a motion picture story is to make things not only logical but visual. You have got to be able to see why someone does this, see why someone goes there.

It is no use telling people: they have got to SEE. We are making pictures, moving pictures, and though sound helps and is the most valuable advance the films have ever made they still remain primarily a visual art.[13]

The nebulous problem of authorship has shaped this essay around the "collective" in the term "collective vision." However, even in Hitchcock's most blue-collar description of collaboration, his focus is on *seeing*. For Hitchcock collaborating and seeing were in essence the same thing. Or perhaps more precisely, "seeing"—the task of showing rather than telling the audience—could not take place without collaboration. As drawings from the preproduction of *Marnie* (1964) and *The Birds* demonstrate (plates 19 and 32), Hitchcock's ability to visualize was impressively developed, especially his talent for picturing different shots and for understanding the effect editing images together would have on the audience. However, when it came to establishing the tone and look of the film from costumes to lighting or writing the story, characters, and dialogue, Hitchcock was profoundly collaborative. An early draft of the *Psycho* (1960) script, for example, has whole sections crossed out and additions, handwritten on smaller yellow paper, inserted into the bound draft. The new dialogue is in scriptwriter Joseph Stefano's handwriting, while the additions of new shots are in Hitchcock's hand.[14]

Director Alfred Hitchcock and playwright Thornton Wilder collaborating,
in Wilder's words, "on the plotting
of the dramatic interest" for *Shadow of
a Doubt* (1943). Still courtesy of the
Academy of Motion Picture Arts and
Sciences. Rights courtesy of Universal
Studios Licensing LLLP.

Director Alfred Hitchcock's cable to his
friend and producer Sidney Bernstein
with an idea for two consecutive shots
in *Under Capricorn* (1949). Courtesy of
the British Film Institute.

COPY OF CABLE FROM MR. HITCHCOCK TO S.L.B. DATED 13/10/48.


        SUDDEN THOUGHT WHAT ABOUT OPENING NIGHT OF

    BALL SEQUENCE BEFORE WE SEE LONG SHOT OF WAITING

    CARRIAGE SCREEN FILLED WITH INVITATION CARDS AND

    ADARE'S HAND LABORIOUSLY FILLING IN BLANK SPACE

    THIS WOULD FADE IN IMMEDIATELY FOLLOWING FLUSKY'S

    WALK AWAY FROM BREAKFAST TABLE STOP WRITING SHOULD

    HAVE CHARACTER OF ADARE AND NOT COPPERPLATE

    THANK YOU

            HITCH

As the draft of the *Psycho* script demonstrates, Hitchcock's filmmaking process—starting with an idea and working toward a finished film—required countless expressions of the re-envisioned idea: countless production sketches, drafts of scripts, storyboards, shot lists, and camera angle diagrams. Each collaborative re-envisioning was practice for the actual filming, which was the ultimate collaborative expression. The film set was where all of the department heads (with the usual exception of the writers and the costume designers) came together to execute the collective vision they had been building during preproduction.

An example of the symbiotic relationship of visualizing and collaborating is a telegram from Hitchcock to Sidney Bernstein (page 10). They were working on *Under Capricorn* (1949) together; Bernstein was producing, Hitchcock was directing. Hitchcock had a "sudden thought" for two shots in the movie and cabled Bernstein for his critical response. Hitchcock did have visions of what his movies should look like, but, in this case and others, they are snippets of the film, a scene here, a sequence there. And those visions were only the point of departure for the further development of a scene or sequence.[15]

The artifacts of these collective visions in the exhibition and book are the focus of *Casting a Shadow*. They demonstrate the visual nature of filmmaking as much as they illuminate its collaborative nature. Whether it is Robert Boyle and Dorothea Holt summarizing *Shadow of a Doubt* (1943) with two powerfully narrative production sketches (plates 23 and 24) or Hitchcock sketching the mise-en-scène for a scene from *North by Northwest* (1959) on the back of a Sheraton Hotel placemat (page 23), these documents are graphic evidence that making movies is a visual art.

Perhaps the most difficult and counterintuitive aspect of authorship in movies is the idea that a director's movie is not his vision but a collective vision—a vision that is shared among the director and his collaborators and eventually synthesized by the director. Indeed, Hitchcock's abilities as a director are more impressive once the shroud of mystification is pulled off. It is in part the aim of

the exhibition and this book to reveal the man in front of the shadow. The objects in the show are images and words from the working processes on Hitchcock's productions. They are therefore not finished products. Although each object has been given a title in this exhibition for the sake of clarity, most did not have titles when they were used in the production. And they are seldom signed and even more rarely dated. Most of the objects require a certain amount of context to be understood, yet once that context is provided, these objects speak for themselves. Whether it is a production design sketch or a rough drawing on a scrap piece of paper, each object has something to say about how the Hitchcock motion picture came to be.

A movie studio is not a factory. In Hitchcock's words, "the filming of each picture is a problem in itself."[16] Yet Hitchcock did have practices, to which, like his oft-repeated themes, he returned. The plate section of this catalogue pulls together the widest possible variety of objects from the breadth of Hitchcock's career. They do not trace any one movie from beginning to end. Instead, the exhibition and the color plates take the objects that are still extant and available and present them as a collage of how the Hitchcock film was created.

The four essays in this catalogue each tackle a different aspect of Hitchcock and motion picture's place in the "household of art." Scott Curtis's essay "The Last Word: Images in Hitchcock's Working Method" deals directly with the exhibition and in particular with the use of sketching in Hitchcock's productions. Curtis offers a taxonomy for organizing the use of drawing. In addition, he delivers a close reading of several objects in the exhibition, interpreting how they may have been used and what their use says about collaboration.

"In and Out of the Frame: Paintings in Hitchcock" by Tom Gunning looks at the use of paintings in many of Hitchcock's films, including *Blackmail* (1929), *The Trouble with Harry* (1955), and *Vertigo* (1958). The implication of Gunning's article is a powerful association between the visual art of painting and filmmaking. Not only do both arts share the frame and the act of looking, paintings in

Hitchcock's movies are often expressions of his characters' hidden emotions. While the exhibition and the plate section describe the importance of visualization in making the Hitchcock film, "In and Out of the Frame" reveals another layer of visualization within the films themselves.

Bill Krohn's essay "*I Confess* and *Nos deux consciences*" is an interpretation of the central theme of *I Confess* (1953) and the writing and rewriting of the script. Krohn's careful reconstruction of the development of the story and the script places an emphasis on the movie's central idea, which as we have seen was of primary importance to Hitchcock and which can be traced through many iterations in other Hitchcock films. Krohn's difficult work uncovering the evolution of a Hitchcock idea is a reminder of one of Hitchcock's central paradoxes. While Hitchcock embraced the "not quite that legitimate"qualities of motion pictures that Robert Warshow described—their mass appeal, their focus on entertainment—he imbued his movies with meaningful ideas for those who choose to think about such things. "*I Confess* and *Nos deux consciences*" maps the development of the script and the idea behind the project, which in the case of *I Confess* was done predominantly with writing.

"Hitchcock à la Carte: Menus, Marketing, and the Macabre" by Jan Olsson details the mélange of Hitchcock's self-promotion and dining habits. Although we mostly remember Hitchcock as the somber master of suspense, much of his press coverage revolved around his eating habits. The inquiring public wanted to know how much Hitchcock weighed, where he dined, and what his favorite foods were. Hitchcock was ever the collaborator, meeting the public halfway and often getting the best of them with his own playful jokes about his size. This is quintessential Hitchcock. He, with the help of writers and publicists, took the bull by the horns and tricked us into believing he and only he was in control of the circumstances.

The articles and images together present a well-rounded picture of Hitchcock and his working relationship with his films and his collaborators.

Throughout his life he refined and reiterated the idea of the Alfred Hitchcock film, making 53 movies in the process and collaborating with scores of people. Only some of them he deemed Hitchcock films—often those that shared his distinctive visual motifs and fascination with certain themes. Creating each one required collaboration and a collective vision.

The beginning of Hitchcock and production designer Robert Boyle's work on *The Birds* is a fitting example. After Hitchcock read Daphne du Maurier's novella, he sent it to Robert Boyle for him to sketch his visual reactions (plate 1). Boyle's drawings, with their eerie foreboding and dramatic restraint, were influential in establishing the movie's tone and production design. They were the first visualization of *The Birds*. Hitchcock, however, was as interested in what Boyle had to say about the idea of *The Birds*. In an interview with Bill Krohn, Boyle recounts their first meeting to discuss the project. It was over lunch. As Boyle remembers it, he spent the lion's share of the meal enumerating to an attentive Hitchcock the reasons *The Birds* was an Alfred Hitchcock movie. Although it seems counterintuitive—that Boyle would explain what makes a Hitchcock film—it marked the beginning of their work on *The Birds*. Hitchcock governed the production, but the creation was a collective process that he shepherded. By studying the artifacts from Alfred Hitchcock film productions we can more precisely understand his creative accomplishments as well as the unique qualities of motion pictures. Hitchcock understood that the new art form of motion pictures was meant for millions of people and that, perhaps, a collective vision is required to successfully make art for such a large number.[17]

2

# The Last Word: Images in Hitchcock's Working Method

SCOTT CURTIS

If we listen to Mr. Hitchcock, we get the distinct impression that he is in total control of every aspect of production, that he plans the film completely—down to the last frame—before he even steps on the set, and that once the film is shot (which at that point is apparently boring for him), there is very little for editors to do except glue the pieces together, so efficient is his shooting style. Here are, for example, some excerpts from conversations between Hitchcock and various interviewers:

Q: *How much of the scripts do you in fact write yourself?*
A: Oh, quite a bit. You see, I used to be a writer myself years ago.[1]

Q: *Is the smallest period involved in production the shooting period?*
A: Oh yes. I wish I didn't have to shoot the picture. When I've gone through the script and created the picture on paper, for me the creative job is done and the rest is just a bore.[2]

Q: *Mr. Hitchcock, what about your editing methods? When do you start to edit your films, and are you able to edit them right through to the very end without anyone else interfering with it?*
A: Well I—following what I have said—do shoot a precut picture. In other words, every piece of film

is designed to perform a function. So therefore, literally, the only type of editing that I do is to tighten up. If a man's coming through a door, going into the room, then you just pull that together by just snippets. But actual creative work in the cutting, for me, is nonexistent, because it is designed ahead of time—precut, which it should be.[3]

Q: *I had understood that you evaded interference by shooting things out of order.*
A: No, I just normally work that way. To me, a picture must be planned on paper. People are always asking me why I don't improvise on the set, and I always reply, "What for? I'd rather improvise in a room with the writer." My method is very simple. I work out a treatment with my screenwriter. In order to do this, you've got to have a visual sense. I never look through the camera; I think only of that white screen that has to be filled up the way you fill up a canvas. That's why I draw rough setups for the cameraman.[4]

Q: *Are you saying that when you see the material [the story], you can visualize the entire movement of that film?*
A: Yes, definitely.
Q: *The whole film?*
A: Beginning to end.
Q: *Could you do that in 1922?*
A: Yes.[5]

15

Peggy Robertson, director Alfred Hitchcock's assistant, with Hitchcock on the set of *Vertigo* (1958). Still courtesy of the Academy of Motion Picture Arts and Sciences. Rights courtesy of Universal Studios Licensing LLLP.

Now, there is certainly a showman in Hitchcock. He was very conscious of his public image, and here we can see that Hitchcock was not above polishing it a bit when given the chance. Of course, there were very good reasons for him to do so, especially since he worked in a town where image is everything. But it was not simply a matter of ego; self-promotion was also a means of job promotion. That is, by demonstrating in interviews and on set that he was able to control or contribute to all aspects of filmmaking, Hitchcock helped to establish himself as someone who could not only direct films but produce them as well. To be able to produce one's film was highly desirable for any director working within the studio system, because it meant far less studio oversight. Hitchcock had constantly battled with producers (such as C. M. Woolf in Great Britain and David O. Selznick in the United States) for creative control and was finally able to produce his own films starting with *Rope* in 1948.

But reading his interviews could give the impression that Hitchcock is amplifying his authorial role in the film at the expense of others, that he is claiming that he did not need the screenwriter or the production designer except to have them execute his preconceived plans. True enough, Hitchcock had his hand in nearly every stage of production and planned extensively during preproduction. It is also true, as we will see, that he had an amazingly visual sense of storytelling. But if we look closely at his production methods, as this exhibition does, we find that accident, improvisation, and collaboration play a much larger role in a Hitchcock production than he would have us believe. It's not that he didn't plan, but film production is so filled with variables that no one, not even Hitchcock, can anticipate them all. Indeed, far from being a nuisance, these variables demanded a technical, problem-solving expertise that Hitchcock not only possessed but thoroughly enjoyed putting to use. But more to the point, a close examination of his production methods reveals that even for Hitchcock, master planner and *auteur extraordinaire*, filmmaking is a fundamentally collaborative enterprise.

The tension between planning and improvisation comes through most clearly when we examine the way Hitchcock and his team used images in the production process. Simply, ideas were *written* and *drawn* before they were photographed. Hitchcock worked with a screenwriter to come up with a written framework (the script), then he worked with a production designer to come up with a visual framework (sketches, storyboards, etc.). These frames indicate the collaborative nature of filmmaking, certainly, but they also speak to the need for improvisation and problem solving on the set. For, despite claims to the contrary, the relation between the script and storyboards and the finished film is not always exact. Consider the use of storyboards, those drawings that map out action in a given scene, sometimes the entire film. On one hand, we have many technicians, assistants, writers, producers, and others attesting to the importance of storyboards for Hitchcock's working method. Each testifies confidently that the storyboards played a vital, even paramount, role in the construction of the film. There might have been some room for improvisation, but very little. "Thank God for the storyboard," assistant editor for *Rear Window* (1954) John Woodcock said. "We even had a copy to assist in the editing."[6] Or take, for another example, this testimony from Hitchcock's longtime assistant, Peggy Robertson, in her oral history with Barbara Hall:

HALL: So a lot of factors that he couldn't have considered in his storyboards he was deciding as you went along?
ROBERTSON: Yes, as we went along. Not many though, the important thing was the storyboard of course.[7]

On the other hand, we have the evidence of the films, which, more often than not, vary considerably from the storyboards. Then there is the fact that Hitchcock did not actually use storyboards for every scene in his films. We also have, as Bill Krohn has demonstrated, evidence from the production records that Hitchcock was not nearly as tied to script or storyboard as the legend would have us believe. There was, for example, much reshooting in *Notorious* (1946), as the story that took shape on the set required retakes of scenes shot at the start of principal photography.[8] In other words, it seems that sometimes the pre-planning was not the end of Hitchcock's creative work on a film.

So what are we to make of this apparent discrepancy in the historical record? We might attribute it to what could be called the "Hitchcock mystique of authorship." As we have seen, Hitchcock gave the impression that he had already made the movie in his head by the time he walked on set, that he had visualized it in storyboards and then merely hung around during principal photography to make sure everything went his way. This is a more or less constant theme in the publicity surrounding Hitchcock, which emphasizes not only the importance of preplanning (and hence storyboards) for his working method, but also his authority as sole creative force behind each film. We might speculate that, caught up in this mystique and myth, Hitchcock's fellow crew members simply overemphasized the importance of storyboards for his films.

But there is another possibility. It could be that we see a discrepancy because we—perhaps led on by the master himself—misunderstand the role of drawings in Hitchcock's method. Maybe when we compare the storyboards with the finished product, expecting one to follow the other, we misunderstand this relationship. I would argue that this is exactly the case: that Hitchcock's storyboards do not always function as a visual contract between director and crew; they are not always a steadfast guide to the visual execution of the film. Moreover, not all drawings for a film are storyboards, and this may be a point of confusion as well. In fact, it is more accurate to say that the drawn images served *multiple* functions for a film, and often different functions from film to film. And this possibility would explain the importance of these images for the various crew members who have commented on them: they saw the sketches so often, in multiple films, contexts, and functions, that the drawings became a visual emblem of Hitchcock's method and authority. The crew saw

the drawings at different points in the process; like the script, they were a constant feature in the production. But unlike a script, they served a variety of functions.

So this essay will sketch out the various kinds of images found in a Hitchcock production (and, by extension, any studio film), but it will also outline how these images functioned. I find that the drawn images in a Hitchcock film served four overlapping functions:

*Brainstorming*
After acquiring a property, Hitchcock would sometimes send it to a trusted production designer, such as Robert Boyle for *The Birds* (1963), and ask him to make some sketches based on his reading of the story (plate 1). These drawings were not meant to be a detailed rendition of each scene in the film. Instead, they were meant to act as a starting point, something to get the conversation started, as it were. They functioned to get the creative process going between director and production designer.

*Communicating*
Sometimes an image did serve to guide the crew. But we must emphasize that it was only a guide, not a firm contract. Scripts were constantly being revised, and images were being revisualized, which helped everyone know exactly what was going on at that stage in the production. Images served as a means of communicating visually what Hitchcock and his principal collaborators had in mind. They also sometimes functioned as directions for executing a specific task, such as a process shot or an insert.

*Problem solving and executing*
Complex scenes, such as the crop-dusting scene in *North by Northwest* (1959), required shot-by-shot planning (plates 56a-d). Hitchcock and his production designer or cinematographer would sketch out the visual elements of the scene beforehand to try to solve knotty problems of camera movement or placement. These could also help the editing along, since they could be easily shuffled and reordered to try out different shot combinations in an era before offline editing.

Pictures spoke to more than the crew. At least since *Saboteur* (1942), studio publicity departments recognized the value of Hitchcock's images for promoting the films. So along with publicity photos of Hitchcock and his crew working, or of scenes in the films, studios would also often include photos of sketches used in the production.

Generally speaking, then, if we look closely at the drawn images in a Hitchcock production, we will find that his sketches and storyboards, rather than eliminating the need for improvisation, actually allowed Hitchcock to be extremely flexible during shooting.

**A Brief Taxonomy**

But first we must categorize the kinds of drawn images one would find in the production process. We can start with images that a director approves, even supervises, but which are primarily the domain of department heads. These include *wardrobe sketches, production and set design drawings*, and *architectural plans*.

*Wardrobe sketches*
Hollywood studios do not buy clothes for their stars "off the rack." They are tailor-made for them. Wardrobe sketches are the designs for these costumes; they are the plans for the character's "look" before the clothes are actually made. Some of the greatest fashion designers—Christian Dior, for example—have contributed wardrobe ideas to feature films. But the best wardrobe designers who worked for the studios—Edith Head, for example, comes immediately to mind—were incredibly versatile in their ability to design costumes for a range of periods and characters (plate 4). In fact, the wardrobe sketch is only nominally created for the tailor and costumer; it also serves to sketch out the character. If "clothes make the man," then we know something more about the nature of the men (and women) in the film by examining the wardrobe sketch. In this respect, these drawings are an important point of collaboration between the wardrobe designer and the director.

*Production and set design drawings*
The same is true for the production or set design. It is often hard to tell the difference between "production design," "art direction," and "set design"; their domains are certainly blurred. Generally speaking, however, "production design" refers to the overall "look" of a film, while "set design" denotes the plans for individual sets. The art director may be in charge of overall production design, but he or she might also be confined to dressing sets, depending on the individual production and studio convention. During the classical Hollywood period, from the 1920s through the 1950s, the art director oversaw production and set design. Later, however, the tasks were sometimes split and we see credits for both production designer and art director. Production design drawings often give more information about the action than set design drawings. Set design drawings suggest the visual pattern of the film—the era, the mood, even the lighting—while providing the set dresser with guidance for such details as furniture style. These drawings can be highly detailed, even painterly renditions, since such things as color can be an important factor in designing the look of the scene. But if we examine production design drawings such as those for Hitchcock's *Shadow of a Doubt* (1943), we see that they indicate not only the style and mood of the film but also specific story action (plates 22–30). In this case, production design drawings are doing much of the work that would later be done by storyboards, which focus on action without much concern for lighting or atmosphere.

*Architectural plans*
But before a room can be dressed or filmed, it must be built. Floor plans are architectural renderings of a set drawn by the production designer. They look very much like blueprints for a house and function in much the same way: as a plan for the construction crew to follow when building the set. There is an important difference, however, as we can see in Henry Bumstead's plans for the sets of *Rebecca* (1940) or Robert Boyle's renderings for the Mount Rushmore house in *North by Northwest*

CONVERTED COTTAGE

Alfred Junge's production design drawing, which focused on set design, of the converted cottage in *Young and Innocent* (1937). Courtesy of the British Film Institute. Copyright: ITV PLC (Granada Int'l)/LFI.

(plate 15). Boyle and Bumstead have drawn the *entire* house, much more than the construction crew actually built. It is very rare for a film production to build an entire house; to save costs they will only build what is needed for any given scene. Why, then, draw such elaborate plans? This points to the multiple functions of even a straightforward blueprint. These plans do more than guide the construction crews; they also map out the "space" of the film. That is, these plans are in some ways architectural fantasies; they are of buildings that will not exist, or exist only "virtually." But they orient everyone who looks at them to the space of the fiction, or what is sometimes called the *diegesis*. This is the fictional world that the characters inhabit. It is a constructed space, of course—anyone who has ever been on a film set can attest to the huge discrepancy between the space of filming and the space of the fiction on screen. But the construction of space is both a practical and psychological matter; it is both physically built and psychologically constructed through editing and camera angles. These architectural plans ostensibly

function not only in a practical sense—to guide the construction crew—but also to map out the fictional space of the film, in the same way that wardrobe sketches tell us about the character.

Set designs and floor plans are generally executed or supervised by department heads. Hitchcock, however, started his career as an art director, so he was not above making his own set designs. It is said, for example, that he did all the designs for *The 39 Steps* (1935). But usually the director only approves these items after creating with the department heads the general principles they need to complete the work for that particular production. Other drawn images, however, are more closely tied to the expertise and vision of the director. These include *camera placement sketches*, *sketches by the director*, and *storyboards*.

*Camera placement sketches*
Sometimes, when the requirements of a particular scene or setting are especially complex, the director and camera person will map out the positions that the camera will occupy as it takes its shots

from different angles. These are, at first glance, very confusing documents, such as the camera plans for *Lifeboat* (1944) (plate 54) or for the crop-dusting sequence in *North by Northwest* (plate 55). The numbers correspond to shot numbers in the continuity script. The angles represent the angle of view each camera will have on the action. These two examples show all the camera positions on one sheet of paper, but it is just as easy to have them on separate pages, as in the camera placement sketches for the kidnapping scene in *North by Northwest* (plates 51–52). The trick is to be able to visualize the shot before placing the camera, including its angle of view and distance from the scene photographed. This is indeed a very difficult task, best left to those with long experience. Occasionally these sketches indicate work that has already been done, as when Robert Burks premeasured the camera distance and angles for most of the shots in *Rear Window*. (Since he was shooting across a courtyard, he did not want to have to measure focal distances every time, so he premeasured distances from specific camera placements.) But the sketches are also often just that—a starting point, though not ultimately a blueprint.

*Sketches by the director*
These kinds of images cover much ground. They can be of anything we have considered so far and more. A director can (and often does) draw a set or a costume or an action to convey his ideas to his crew. Generally, the sketches by Hitchcock in this collection are his attempts to visualize a scene by drawing it out, so to speak. Consider, for example, his drawings from *Saboteur* (plate 50). These are sketches of the Statue of Liberty sequence, in which the two antagonists battle it out on the statue's torch. Hitchcock here draws the action by sketching figures in successive poses, in an almost chronophotographic rendition of the movement. But note also that he uses those same drawings to mark out within the scene possibilities for analytical editing. That is, within one frame, which might indicate a long shot, he will mark with a dashed line the potential for a cut-in to a medium shot. Rather than drawing successive shots, as in a storyboard, Hitchcock here draws the action from

a single vantage point and then marks off the shots within that point of view. In other words, he adopts the chronophotographic style in this sketch (having all the action within one frame) for both the depiction of movement and for the camera distance. This approach works as a kind of efficient shorthand to guide his crew.

*Storyboards*
Storyboards are often the most visually compelling images in a production, not only because of their quality but because they depict action. This is what distinguishes a storyboard from a set design sketch; one depicts the action, the *story*, while the other confines itself to depicting the space alone. While the director might sketch out his ideas for a scene, usually the storyboard is a more detailed rendition from a capable graphic artist. Hitchcock had considerable drawing talent, but he would still leave the task of creating storyboards to other hands, usually graphic artists or production designers. (Dorothea Holt, John De Cuir, and Harland Frazer were among the talented artists who worked with Hitchcock on storyboards, under the supervision of art department heads, such as Robert Boyle.) But the storyboards were created in close collaboration with Hitchcock and his screenwriter. After reading the script and consulting with the director, the storyboard artist would present a visual interpretation of the scene, sometimes shot by shot. These images were not created for the entire film, however. While Hitchcock is known for his storyboards, he used them only for particular scenes, or for all scenes when the film required special planning, such as the technically challenging *Lifeboat*. The same is true for studio filmmaking in general: *Gone with the Wind* (1939) was completely storyboarded, but historically speaking only animated films were consistently boarded from beginning to end. These days more and more directors are opting for the storyboard, not only because the technical complexity of special-effects-laden films requires it, but because it provides more authorial control. But to understand the role of the storyboard, we must examine in detail the way it functions in a Hitchcock production.

## The Multiple Functions of Images

*Brainstorming*

Once Hitchcock acquired a property, he started to visualize how it would look on the screen. Despite his claim above that he could "visualize the entire movement" of the film immediately and all at once, visualization was an ongoing process. It would be more accurate to say that Hitchcock was *always* visualizing from the time that he encountered the story. Preplanning of this sort was not just a Hitchcock quirk, however; he had been trained to do this. Take, for example, this rider on a contract for an early Hitchcock feature, *The Skin Game* (1931):

This Scenario has been agreed by the Director and the Company's Scenario Editor. No alterations are to be made therein during the shooting, i.e. no scenes not outlined are to be shot.

Should the Director consider that any alteration is necessary before shooting, this should be a subject for discussion, and agreement with the Scenario Editor, and if any alterations are agreed upon they should be noted in detail and on this Scenario and initialed by both Director and Scenario Editor.

Failure by the Director to comply with these regulations will be regarded as a departure from the Company's express instructions, and therefore, a breach of his contract with the Company.[9]

We do not know how seriously such breaches were taken, but assuming they were taken seriously, we can see the enormous pressure the director was under to get the script in shape before shooting began. This kind of pressure almost required that the director preplan and visualize each scene before it was filmed.

Visualization began, then, right away. For example, in preparation for *The Birds*, Hitchcock gave his production designer, Robert Boyle, a copy of the Daphne du Maurier novella and asked Boyle to draw some sketches from it (plate 1). Boyle crafted some general visual ideas, which were a starting point for conversation between Boyle and Hitchcock about the look and mood of the film. This probably happened even before Hitchcock met with the screenwriter, Evan Hunter, to discuss the story. The sketches themselves indicate that Boyle visualized how an attack might be framed and broken into separate shots—especially how the menace of the birds might be conveyed visually, through shadows and reaction shots. These sketches do not have much resemblance to the finished film, but they were not meant as strict guides for filming. Instead, the sketches were intended as an exercise to begin to articulate the intricacies of this production and what its special features might require.

On the other end of the spectrum, we have Hitchcock's own sketches, which he made at various points in the production as he grappled with translating the script into visuals. These sketches are much less detailed than Boyle's drawings, as we might expect. Hitchcock sometimes drew on the back pages of scripts as a way of visualizing scenes or figuring out specific problems as he was reading. The sketches on one of the scripts for *Torn Curtain* (1966) serve as a good example of this type of image (plate 21). Here Hitchcock might be drawing out the action dictated by the script as a way of capturing the corresponding image in his head. But these drawings could also function as a way of comparing the directions contained within the script with his own experience and vision of how it would play out in front of the camera. Or the sketch could also work as a means of communicating to his cameraman even more specifically the framing he wants for this particular shot. Indeed, a sketch such as this one probably works in all of these ways at the same time.

If Boyle's *Birds* sketches betray a wealth of consideration and graphic skill, they also demonstrate the luxury of time, having been drawn well before principal photography. Even Hitchcock's *Torn Curtain* sketches were probably drawn before actual filming began. But some visualization takes place at the spur of the moment, even on the set or during production. A good example of this kind of image is Hitchcock's sketch of the cafeteria scene in *North by Northwest*. Hitchcock himself drew this sketch on the back of a Sheraton Hotel placemat. We do not know exactly where or when this sketch

Director Alfred Hitchcock's sketch of the cafeteria scene in *North by Northwest* (1959). Courtesy of the Academy of Motion Picture Arts and Sciences. Rights courtesy of Warner Bros. NORTH BY NORTHWEST © Turner Entertainment Co. A Warner Bros. Entertainment Company. All Rights Reserved.

was made, but we can assume it came at some point during the shooting. Here Hitchcock is trying to visualize a scene in which the character is shot —how will the action be blocked? (That is, how will the actors be placed within the shot?) How does the scene resolve itself? The sketch figure in bold on the right fires the gun (note the movement of the bullet indicated by the dotted line), and Hitchcock indicates the character's escape with the arrow pointing to the door. The scene seems simple enough—why sketch it out? There are any number of choices that must be made even for a straightforward scene such as this. But we must also keep in mind that the act of sketching is itself a way of thinking in images and solving problems. We do not know the circumstances of the sketch— it might have been made in answer to a specific question his cameraman, say, had about how the scene would move. It might have been drawn to emphasize a particular point in the action that needed someone's attention. Or it might have been a doodle that Hitchcock made to busy himself while he waited for his steak. But the sketch demonstrates not only how the ambiguity of images allows them to function in a variety of ways, but also how sketching is a way of generating ideas while grasping the action and getting a firm grip on the movement of the film.

*Communicating*

Unless Hitchcock *was* doodling while waiting for his steak, most images were drawn to communicate something to someone, usually a succinct "it should look like this." But making these images was always in itself a matter of communication and collaboration. Hitchcock communicated what should be in the image, but there was always some collaboration in the execution of the drawing, an interaction between word and image, between script and storyboard. For example, as *Psycho* (1960) was being rewritten, Hitchcock wrote visual descriptions with each new rewrite of a scene. That is, Hitchcock wrote out in words what he wanted visually in each drawn image.[10] Talking, writing, and drawing are all part of the process of generating visual ideas. The visualization process almost demands the alternation of word and image. On one hand, the ambiguous image sometimes requires words to stabilize its meaning. On the other hand, words cannot compete with the efficiency of the image in conveying information quickly and precisely. This back-and-forth between images and words is inherently collaborative, since Hitchcock cannot describe in words *everything* that goes into an image, even one as schematic as a storyboard. So the artist must make choices about the framing, angle, lighting, mood, or any number of variables in his or her construction of the image. These choices, in turn, feed back into the overall visualization of the film as choices to be acted upon. Storyboard images are often not definitive—they rarely match the final shot detail for detail—but they are part of the conversation that creates that final shot.

We can take a closer look at the conversation between Hitchcock and his collaborators by examining his instructions for storyboarding certain sequences in *The Birds*. In the Hitchcock Papers at the Margaret Herrick Library at the Academy of Motion Picture Arts and Sciences, there are two intriguing lists of shots, handwritten by Hitchcock on yellow notepaper, that correspond to storyboard images of the scenes (plates 31–32). The "Tides attack" and the "Crow sequence" are sequences in which birds attack the townspeople of Bodega Bay. These lists were probably created in a meeting with production designer Boyle after Hunter had turned in the final draft of his script.[11] The lists were needed because the Hunter script did not provide—nor was it intended to provide— shot-by-shot descriptions of the scenes. From the script Hitchcock and Boyle came up with a first draft, in the form of these notes, of what it actually would look like on screen. Then they gave the list to Harold Michelson to draw into storyboards. Here's a sample from the "Crow sequence," in which Melanie (Tippi Hedren) arrives at the schoolhouse playground to find crows massing menacingly on the jungle gym:

18. The play yard full of crows.
19. Big head of horrified Melanie.
20. The play yard.
21. Big profile of Melanie. She turns with back to camera and goes toward the school looking across at crows as she goes away. The camera follows her for a few paces and then it stops so that her image becomes smaller as she goes up the steps into the school.
22. A side-on dolly shot of the crows to cut into the first part of #21. After this, follow existing script for school interiors.
23. A full shot—straight on of all the crows, say, 6 feet long.

24. A nearer shot and another angle of #23. 8 feet long.
25. Closer still and a different angle to #23 and #24. 10 feet.
26. A low angle of 5 or 6 crows filling the screen. 12 feet.
27. A full screen of crows—about 50 or more— the shout off [offscreen]—the feet pattering. Suddenly the crows rise—the camera pans up with them.[12]

It's beautiful to see how efficiently Hitchcock visualizes a scene. Throughout his papers there are many such examples, from transcripts of conversations between Hitchcock and his team, that demonstrate that he was always thinking first of the way a scene would look on screen.[13] (Sometimes, as in the famous "bird's-eye view" shot of the attack at the Tides restaurant, Hitchcock's vision took considerable effort to realize.)[14] But the point is that, first, Hitchcock visualized *in conversation* with others—either his screenwriter or his production designer, or both. His visual ideas usually came as a result of developing the script and storyboards with others. Hitchcock was good at visualizing a film, but it never happened in a vacuum. He did not think up a film from the beginning to the end once he found a story. Or, if he did, it was only a skeletal construction that filled out and came to life in conversation with others. If he was good at visualizing without a script, he was *very* good at taking story ideas from writers and making them better. He did not simply dictate his ideas, either, but was happy to use good suggestions. For example, in the attack at the children's birthday party in *The Birds*, Boyle suggested that the children play "blind man's bluff" and that the girl is attacked when blindfolded; this suggestion made it into the script and eventually into the film.[15] Hitchcock might give the impression that he dictated the scripts, but the truth is that he needed screenwriters and designers and cameramen every step of the way to sharpen, enhance, and even rework his ideas.[16]

Secondly, this list shows the way in which words and images worked together and demonstrates that storyboards, and even documents such as this list, had multiple functions. This is not only a list of shots to be storyboarded, but a list of shots to be filmed and edited. Note that Hitchcock makes shooting suggestions at this early stage: one shot of the crows should be "6 feet long" and the last in that set should be "12 feet" to compound the suspense of the scene. But this is not, as some have suggested, a shot list made for the editor, since it clearly suggests movements and angles as if the shots did not exist yet.[17] Instead, the shot lengths are suggestions for the cameraman, but they also work as a shorthand for Hitchcock to indicate the mood of the scene, the suspense as it builds, which is translated visually by storyboard artist Harold Michelson. But with such an efficient written list of visuals, why storyboard this sequence at all? Hitchcock decides to storyboard crucial, climactic sequences precisely because they are so important to the suspense of the film. Yes, he relies on the expertise of his department heads, and especially of his production designer and director of photography, but storyboards are also important to communicate more accurately to his camera team what Hitchcock wants the image to look like on film.

But storyboards are subject to revision, too. The best example of "revisualization" before production is the Statue of Liberty storyboard sequence for *Saboteur* (plates 44–49).[18] This sequence, the climactic finale of the film, features a struggle between the protagonists on the statue. We have three sets of sketches: two sets by artist John De Cuir and one set by Hitchcock. It is fairly clear that the two De Cuir sets—one set of 14 all on one page, and another set of larger, more detailed images—come one after the other. The larger images appear to be revisions of the smaller images in the other set. The role of Hitchcock's sketches, however, is not clear. They roughly correspond to some, but not all, of the images. So they could either come before or between the De Cuir sets. That is, they could be initial suggestions for the storyboard images, or they could be suggestions for revision. In any case, the images are obviously being revised at least twice, especially in terms of camera angle. Notice that the last set of De Cuir images emphasizes the alternation of dizzyingly high and low angles, which Hitchcock adopted in the scene as it appears in the film. Hitchcock communicates his visual ideas in two ways, with words and, as we see in this example, images. But there is always an interplay between the two; in the gap between them, revision and collaboration take place.

*Problem solving and executing*
Storyboards and sketches are used not only to visualize a scene, but also to identify and solve technical problems related to the filming of the scene. Take, for example, the "Cypress Point" sequence storyboard from *Vertigo* (1958) (plates 42–43). In this scene Scottie (James Stewart) and Madeleine (Kim Novak) have driven out to Cypress Point to talk things over. The storyboard shows the action in the scene, but in the examples from Hitchcock's papers, we have additional information: "Sc. 185 EXT. CYPRESS POINT (DAY). Madeleine stands alone silhouetted against the sky. Camera pans over to Scottie in car watching. Location with doubles." And "Sc. 185A. Scottie sits in car watching her. She does not move. Transp. plus car."[19] These storyboards indicate the position of body doubles and of the back projection that would be filmed in the studio. So scene 185 requires location shooting with doubles, while scene 185A requires back projection in the studio with a car in the foreground. In this respect the sketches serve as a kind of reminder to the filmmakers of where they are and what will be needed. Storyboard images can be separated and rearranged, like a deck of cards, to accommodate different aspects of production, from principle photography to second-unit work.

Special-effects work often requires a storyboard as an aid to advance planning. We have two examples from *Marnie* (1964). In the first, storyboards are drawn to indicate the special effects needed: the "racetrack and hunting" sequence requires a shot of "C.U. Marnie–enjoys–ride–Plate X-425 A-Z (rocking horse) Process."[20] This means that shot 425 is going to require a mechanical horse for actress Tippi Hedren to ride in the studio, and that the background containing riders and horses will be either back-projected in the studio or matted in during postproduction. Other than the caption, however, we would not know that this is a special-effects shot. In the other example, however, the image itself is a guide for the effect. In "Study for Matte," Boyle, or a member of his design team, has sketched a scene and then outlined in red ink the part of the frame that will be replaced by a matte painting (plate 12). In this effect, a portion of the setting is filmed (in this case, the house and paths in the foreground) and a matte—cut exactly to fit the rest of the picture—is placed over the other part of the setting to create a blank space on the film. This space will be filled in during post production by superimposing a painting (or another photograph) that has been drawn to fit the matte exactly. In this way, filmmakers do not have to settle for locations as they are—they can create their own. But the sketch in this case has a very precise problem-solving and execution function.

Such is also the case with camera placement sketches, which help solve complex logistical problems and serve as a guide to filming the scene. The most famous example here would be the crop-dusting scene from *North by Northwest*.[21] Here the visualization that Hitchcock worked out with his collaborators takes two forms: the continuity, which is a written list of shots (plates 56a–d), as in the example from *The Birds* above; and a camera placement sketch (plate 55). Unlike a storyboard, which renders each shot as a separate image, this sketch shows all the shots of the sequence at once in an overhead schematic view. The numbers on the sketch correspond to the shot numbers in the continuity, and the angles indicate the camera's angles of view. The circled *T* stands for the position of Thornhill, while the other outlined *T*s at the top and bottom of the sketch represent the airplane. Planning it in this way not only helps articulate what is needed for the scene, but it also insures that the scene is shot efficiently—shots 20, 22, 24, 26F, and 32, for example, need to be filmed from the same position, according to this scheme.

Dear Dolores:

Please excuse the informality of this letter -- but I don't have a secretary and so have to rough it. I'm sending most of the stills we're ordering from "North by Northwest" -- with a few more to be sent your way as soon as they come up from the lab.

In addition, I'm sending about 13 stills from which I would like Mr. Hitchcock to make the sketches I discussed with him before he left for Europe. As a reminder, they are for Coronet magazine -- and theoretically sketches he made before the scenes were filmed. This is for a layout in which his sketches and the resultant scenes would be compared, to show how he maps out every detail of his productions before the scenes are photographed.

From these stills (the 13) please keep any which you might want to use to illustrate his script, in addition to the others.

Appreciate your help and hope to hear from you soon when Mr. Hitchcock can see us -- anywhere at his convenience -- to do a tape transcription we have written and to discuss "North by Northwest" exploitation.

Best as ever --

Rick
Rick Ingersoll

An undated memo from publicist Rick Ingersoll
requesting that storyboards for *North by
Northwest* (1959) be made after shooting was
completed in order "to show how [Hitchcock]
maps out every detail of his productions."
Courtesy of the Academy of Motion Picture Arts
and Sciences. NORTH BY NORTHWEST © Turner
Entertainment Co. A Warner Bros. Entertainment Company. All Rights Reserved.

*Publicizing*

Regarding the filming of this sequence, Boyle said, "For certain sequences like Mount Rushmore or Phillip Vandamm's house we did storyboards, but we were moving so fast on that production that we didn't have time to do them for the crop-dusting sequence."[22] So how do we explain the storyboards that we do have from the crop-dusting sequence? A letter in the Hitchcock Papers from Rick Ingersoll, a publicist, sheds some light:

In addition, I'm sending about 13 stills from which I would like Mr. Hitchcock to make the sketches I discussed with him before he left for Europe. As a reminder, they are for Coronet magazine— and theoretically sketches he made before the scenes were filmed. This is for a layout in which his sketches and the resultant scenes would be compared, to show how he maps out every detail of his productions before the scenes are photographed.[23]

So it seems that the sketches made for this sequence were part of a sly move to maintain Hitchcock's image as a master planner, as the sole architect of his films. Yet if we examine these images closely, we see a fundamental irony in the way they are being used. First, even though Hitchcock did not map out every detail of his films before they were photographed, the publicity department is using these storyboards to support that claim, when they actually support the opposite: that they are part of an ongoing visualization process that is both improvisational and collaborative. The publicity department doesn't really care how these images were actually used, of course— the publicists have their own goals that may or may not coincide with the facts of film history. Yet these *North by Northwest* sketches, surprisingly, do not match the finished film as they were designed to do. It is indeed ironic that images— drawn after the fact—designed to uphold Hitchcock's control over the film end up looking more like the provisional images that storyboard images really are. They were not even drawn by Hitchcock, further undermining the claims to sole authorship that they were made to support, yet ultimately

reflecting the way storyboard images are actually made. So the whole endeavor seems incongruous: it tries to fool us into thinking one thing (Hitchcock as sole creator) and ends up confirming the opposite.

But we must also look at the bigger picture: the publicity department's efforts in themselves also indicate that making a Hitchcock film was always about making a "Hitchcock" as well. Two images were being constructed: the film and the public persona of the director. Both required collaboration. Storyboards were made to generate a vision of the film, but they were also used to generate a vision of Hitchcock the director. In other words, the entity we know as "Hitchcock" was a construction as well, the superimposition of a variety of different "images," from his famous profile to his cameos to his interviews to the use of these storyboards in a publicity campaign. And even though Hitchcock was very conscious of his public persona from early in his career, this public image was one that he could not have created entirely on his own; indeed, the nature of that kind of work fits neatly with the expertise of studio publicity departments. So the final irony is that this use of storyboards to give the impression of authorial control—an aspect also latent in the use of storyboards in the production process—only reveals that impression to be ultimately the result of collaboration anyway. Of course, Hitchcock *was* the director—he was Hitchcock, after all, and as such, he always had the last word. But Hitchcock's last word—his sketches, his films, his persona—was an image that he couldn't have created without the help of others.

# 3

# In and Out of the Frame: Paintings in Hitchcock

TOM GUNNING

Hitchcock's mastery of cinematic framing beckons to us from nearly every shot of his films. His visual style turns on careful consideration of where to place characters and objects within the filmic frame, the precise accent given by lighting, the shaping of space through his selection of lenses, his use of color as a means of attracting attention and creating visual relations, and a dynamic sense of how frames interact through editing or become transformed through movement within the frame —or the movement of the camera itself. Careful attention to Hitchcock's use of sketches and storyboards for the preparation of his filming reveals his system of plotting his shots as the act of framing and the staging of action within a frame. But beyond regulating the components of his visual style, the frame also plays an important thematic role in his films, especially when he used an interior compositional frame, such as a window or a doorway, within the larger film frame. Although the meaning and use of such a frame varies from film to film, certain patterns are recurrent, derived often from his use of the thriller genre, such as the entrapment of characters. Other uses of such frames within frames relate to Hitchcock's stylistic use of point of view, underscoring the act of looking, as in the many views through the window or camera lenses central to one of his masterpieces, *Rear Window* (1954).

In addition to his use of windows and doorways, Hitchcock also used compositional frames to invoke the other arts, especially theater and painting. From his earliest films Hitchcock used stage prosceniums and paintings as ways of framing significant elements, endowing them with additional importance or ambiguity. Theater and painting also represent for Hitchcock concentrations of the gaze and therefore make reference to such themes as voyeurism, masquerade, desire, and deception. In this essay I will trace the interrelation between paintings (or their reproductions), their frames (or edges), and the frame of Hitchcock's camera. This is not precisely virgin territory. Hitchcock's relation to the arts has been the subject of two exhibition catalogues and of an elegant and insightful essay by Brigitte Peucker, included in her book *The Material Image.*[1] My treatment certainly overlaps with those earlier considerations, especially with Peucker's. However, my focus (or my frame) is a bit narrower. I am looking precisely at the way the formal aspects of painting, the differentiation between the space of representation and the space of the world of the observer, are both kept apart and interrelated.[2] Paintings in Hitchcock rarely play a merely decorative role. Instead, through their dynamic relation to the act of framing, they project an influence into the world of the character as conduits of guilt and desire.

## Warm and Real, or Cold and Lonely?
## Works of Art in Hitchcock

Let's begin at some apparent distance from our theme, with a song overheard in one of Hitchcock's greatest films, *Rear Window*. Like *The Birds* (1963), *Rear Window* lacks a conventional musical score; instead it features a carefully arranged aural accompaniment composed from the sounds that drift into the Greenwich Village apartment of L. B. Jefferies (James Stewart) during a pre-air-conditioning summer, when windows were left open and the street, back courtyard, and even fire escapes buzzed with noise and activity. This urban cacophony includes snatches of music (an eclectic mix of Leonard Bernstein, Béla Bartók, Rodgers and Hart, and hits from recent Paramount films, such as Dean Martin's "That's Amore"). Although this sound tapestry supposedly derives from contingent neighborhood activities, Hitchcock carefully matches them to events of the film, providing accompaniment as well as counterpoint. Central to these musical fragments, and behaving very much like a soundtrack theme song, is the tune "Lisa" (not so coincidentally, named for the leading lady of the film, played by Grace Kelly), which is composed by one of Jefferies's neighbors, the songwriter (played by Ross Bagdasarian). Following Hitchcock's interest in portraying processes that develop parallel to the plot of his films, this song progresses from rough and halting improvisation on a piano, to a chamber music version (counterpointing Lisa's adventurous foray into Thorwald's apartment), to the final demo recording complete with lyrics that we hear over the film's denouement.

But there is another musical ode to Lisa tucked away in *Rear Window*, like so many *trouvées* in this film, as Hitchcock stuffs potential significance into every cranny of the courtyard beyond Jefferies's rear window. Detective Tom Doyle (Wendell Corey) has just left Jeff's apartment, deflating Lisa and Jeff's theories that cross-courtyard neighbor Lars Thorwald (Raymond Burr) has murdered his wife. Somberly, the couple look out their window at the apartment of the neighbor Jeff has

dubbed "Miss Lonely Heart" (Judith Evelyn). This unmarried middle-aged woman has brought home a young man, who proceeds to put the moves on her quite aggressively. This rather unromantic scene becomes aurally counterpointed as the guests at a party taking place in the songwriter's apartment on the other side of the courtyard begin singing another hit song from a recent Paramount film, "Mona Lisa," which had won the Academy Award a few years earlier, with a popular version sung by Nat King Cole. The sad and tawdry tryst reaches its abrupt ending as we hear the lyrics drifting across the courtyard:

Many dreams have been brought to your doorstep
They just lie there, and they die there
Are you warm, are you real, Mona Lisa
Or just a cold and lonely, lovely work of art?

The song echoes and anticipates the film's theme song "Lisa" (although Hitchcock indicated his own dissatisfaction with Franz Waxman's song, and it certainly never gained the Academy Award or the popularity of "Mona Lisa"). The question these lyrics pose to the painting echoes Jefferies's own sense that his Lisa remains somehow too aesthetic and remote ("that rarified atmosphere of Park Avenue"), too lovely and cold.

*Rear Window* presents a rather perverse romance: the story of a man overcoming his reluctance towards sex and marriage by learning to incorporate his mistress (a lesson, I should add, that she, herself, teaches him) into his fantasies of murder and detection. Lisa ceases to be the distant, fetishized image of beautiful display (typified by her role as a fashion mannequin) and becomes an active "serial queen" heroine: digging in the garden at night in search of dead bodies; climbing into an apartment and diving in the window to gain evidence; and finally being subjected to a beating by the villain and to arrest by the police.[3] Jefferies's intensely erotic response to Lisa after her tangle with Thorwald leaves no doubt that his passion has been rekindled. To describe Jefferies (as is often done) simply as a voyeur leaves out most of the story: to become truly excited, this Peeping Tom demands a narrative frame for his vision. One

could say that Hitchcock heats up Jefferies's heterosexual passion by moving Mona Lisa from her remote and statically posed frame and placing her within the more dynamic frame of an action film in a self-reflexive scenario of danger and punishment, whose meta-psychological implications were detailed decades ago by Laura Mulvey in her classic description of Hitchcock's plots.[4]

Although *Rear Window* abounds with frames, and frames within frames, for the most part these refer to the mobile frames of photography and cinematography, rather than the framed and still images of painting (even the still photographs constantly referenced in the film seem more important as indices of motion, the racing car wheel that caused Jefferies's injury careening at the camera, or of change, the slide image of the garden where the differing height of the flowers reveals that something has been dug up). With one minor exception, which I will return to later, paintings play little role in this film. However, painting (and the frame that defines its images) plays a major role in Hitchcock's work as a whole, one that frequently raises "Mona Lisa's" questions about the relation the painted image bears to both reality

and the warmth of desire. Hitchcock's fascination with portraits of women always raises the question of the power an image can exert on those outside the frame and, therefore, the image's ability to exceed its static and framed existence. Thus the static image offered by a painting poses a crisis for Hitchcock, one evoking suspended desire contending with potentially deadly malevolence. Without aspiring to be exhaustive, I will attempt to survey in this essay the key role painting plays in Hitchcock's films: framing frozen images suspended between desire and death; as the expression of guilt; and finally as the opening of a passage into another scene beyond the frame.

### The Deadly Living Image

The earliest significant paintings in Hitchcock's cinema succinctly prefigure themes that later films will unfold. When, in *The Lodger* (1927), Ivor Novello as the mysterious lodger is shown by Daisy's mother (Marie Ault) the room he intends to rent, he reacts with unexpected alarm to the vaguely pre-Raphaelite pictures of women with abundant blonde hair. Hitchcock's camera responds to the images as well, tracking along the walls. The proud landlady is taken aback by her new tenant's negative reaction to her flair for interior decoration. He asks that the pictures be removed, which she agrees to somewhat reluctantly. In later scenes in the lodger's room, the former pictures have left signs of their absence, pale oblongs where they once hung and shielded the wallpaper from dust or sunlight. The lodger's excessive reaction to the pictures provides another instance of the lodger's mysterious behavior that progressively makes him a suspect in the Jack the Ripper-type murders of young blonde women occurring in this London neighborhood. We learn eventually, of course, that he is not the murderer but rather an avenger, the brother of the murderer's first victim, trying to track her killer. This role provides Hitchcock's first developed instance of moral ambiguity based in ambiguous identifications, since the anonymous killer has taken precisely "The Avenger" as his epithet, proclaimed in notes he attaches to his victims like an artist's signature. If suspicion of the lodger proves unfounded, the series of connections between him and the Avenger reveals the ambiguity and possible perversity of the lodger's obsession with (and possibly identification with) his sister's murderer. In retrospect, therefore, we recognize the pictures of blonde women as triggers for the lodger's traumatic memory, multiple reproductions of his dead sister, a multiplication also reflected in the Avenger's serial victims. The attempt to repress these memories by removing the pictures from the wall cannot eradicate their indelible traces, sinister reminders alerting us that in Hitchcock such images carry a power beyond the merely pictorial: the ability to imprint themselves on a consciousness even when apparently removed from view.

Hitchcock's films feature a number of pivotal portraits of women, developing the themes adumbrated in The Lodger's erotic obsession, traumatic memory, and thwarted attempts at repression. Hitchcock's treatment of portraits of dead women follows in the tradition of Edgar Allan Poe's "The Oval Portrait" (and romantic and gothic fiction)—a transfer of life energy from the subject of the portrait to the portrait itself, so that the portrait seems to possess a vital energy even after (perhaps especially after) the death of the subject herself.[5] Thus, in Rebecca (1940), the second Mrs. de Winter (Joan Fontaine) follows the sinister suggestion of housekeeper Mrs. Danvers (Judith Anderson) and agrees to come to a costume ball in a dress modeled on the portrait of a family ancestor, Caroline de Winter, that hangs at the head of the stairs of the family mansion, Manderley. Such imitation of a painting by a human figure invokes the tradition of the tableau vivant, a living picture. However, when she descends the stairway in this costume before the ball, passing the portrait itself, which she checks expectantly (although most of the massive painting remains beyond the frame of this shot), her appearance does not recall an image come to life as much as the influence of the dead reaching out and ensnaring the living. Her appearance as a living picture causes Max's sister (Gladys Cooper) to gasp the name of the deceased first Mrs. de Winter, "Rebecca," as husband Max (Laurence Olivier) recoils in anger and orders her to take the costume off—an even more intense negative reaction than that of the lodger to the blonde beauties hung along his wall, but amounting to the same attempt at repression. It is revealed that the former Mrs. de Winter wore precisely such a costume, reproducing the portrait, at an earlier ball. Thus the "realization" of the portrait that hangs in the stairway expresses Rebecca's continued power over Manderley and her former husband and her baleful influence on his young bride.[6] As Peucker nicely puts it, "It is not the ancestral portrait that is brought to life, in other words, but the dead Rebecca who had worn this same costume to an earlier ball."[7] Instead of bringing an ancient ancestor to life, this masquerade reduces the young bride to a facsimile of the dead wife, draining away her own life and identity.

While Hitchcock always remains on the Anne Radcliffe side of the gothic romance, rationalizing the apparent supernatural as the psychological effects of ambiguous perceptual stimuli, these portraits of dead women embody a ghostly influence, the persistence of a fatal power not only beyond repression but beyond the barrier of death itself. In true gothic tradition, the portraits embody a survival after death; nonetheless the effect on the living remains deadly. In *Vertigo* (1958), Hitchcock created the most complete and complex fashioning of this theme. The portrait of Carlotta Valdes provides an essential prop in the plot of Gavin Elster (Tom Helmore) to murder his wife (and, incidentally, destroy the sanity of his former college chum, Scottie Ferguson [James Stewart]). The sequence in the gallery of the San Francisco Legion of Honor in which Scottie finds the woman he takes to be Madeleine Elster (Kim Novak) seated entranced before the *Portrait of Carlotta* shows Hitchcock's mastery of doubling of image and meaning. This woman seated intently before a painting enacts Madeleine's obsession with her dead ancestor, whose portrait transfixes her gaze, following the story Elster has fed Scottie. As the camera frames Madeleine from Scottie's position, her back is turned to us, a sign of her absorption in the image before her and of his observation of her. Although the composition conveys her gaze at the painting, it is Scottie's viewpoint that is given to us, as Scottie's own growing obsession with Madeleine/Carlotta takes center stage, mirroring Madeleine's supposed fantasy of possession.

Hitchcock uses camera movement to convey the force of a look: two dolly-ins place us within Scottie's gaze, which is concentrated on the relation between Madeleine and the portrait. Thus Scottie's fascination with the woman's own obsession with the portrait sets up a *mise en abyme* of gazes: Scottie watches Madeleine's stare at the canvas, as the camera movement expresses his gaze and ends up merging the living woman with the subject of the painting. The tracking shots that link Madeleine and the portrait first draw a series of simple comparisons. The camera dollies from the floral bouquet Madeleine holds to the identical one held by Carlotta. Likewise the camera moves from the spiraling arrangement of Madeleine's hairdo to Carlotta sporting the same curl in the portrait. Yet the camera movement seems excessive if Hitchcock only intended to draw this com-

parison. A simple cut between the painted and the real hairdos and bouquets would make the relation clear, whereas the dolly-in camera makes us gradually approach the painting, finally drawing so close to its surface we feel we could touch it. There is more involved in this elegant scene than a detective noticing significant details. Through the dolly-in, the camera seems to sink into and open up the space of the painting, not only directing Scottie's (and our) attention, but seemingly confusing the space of observer and painting, of representation and reality. However, the closer we get, the more the flatness of the painting, a barrier to our penetration, asserts itself. We must linger over this paradox, because it lies at the core of Hitchcock's use of the painting and its frame.

The frame of a painting represents its aesthetic autonomy. Since the mastering of perspective and the development of easel painting, artists in this tradition have aspired to create self-contained representations that retain a strong visual resemblance to our visual experience while remaining separate from our world. The frame cuts the painting off from the surrounding world, funnels and directs the audience's viewpoint into the perspectival scheme of the painting. It works on a double logic: first separating its image from surrounding space, and second aesthetically (that is, *playfully*— we aren't dealing with literal illusions here) allowing the spatial order of the tableau to command the viewer's attention, creating a fantasy of a window or portal onto another world. This sets up the most basic contradiction of the perspectival system, an invitation to the viewer to visually enter the world of the painting, while realizing the impossibility of actual physical penetration. Hitchcock's track forward into the *Portrait of Carlotta* plays with the fantasy of entering the world of the image, inviting *and* denying it simultaneously in a manner that a mere cut to an enlarged detail (as in an analytical illustration in an art history textbook) could not accomplish. We approach and are barred simultaneously. In *Vertigo* (and, as I will show, in *Blackmail* [1929]) Hitchcock moves his camera so that the frame of the shot interacts dynamically with the frame (or the edges of the

canvas in *Blackmail*) of a painting. Moving back and revealing the limits of the painting, it reveals it as an image. When the frame of a shot moves within the limits of the painting, the subject of the painting seems almost to overwhelm the film, to enter into the space of the film and dwell among the characters.

\*

If the fantasy of entering a painting occurs commonly in the average observer's relation to perspectival painting, Hitchcock (and the gothic tradition that he continually refers to, revises, and renews) also invokes its uncanny complement, the idea of the emergence of the subject from within the frame of the painting into the space of the observer. The fantasy of bodily emergence from the space of representation evokes more readily the frame of photography and the cinema (examples include the wheel coming towards the camera in Jeff's photographs in *Rear Window*, but also the *topos* in early cinema of trains rushing towards the viewer; the devices of 1950s 3-D movies; and, more recently, the video visitant of *The Ring*). In contrast to these invasive photographic and cinematic shocks, emergence from the portrait in the gothic tradition has less physical impact. Instead the gothic tradition invokes the uncanny power of a portrait's gaze, such as the fascination exerted by portraits that seem to look back at the viewer, or whose eyes even follow them around the room.[8] Thus in this gallery sequence Madeleine seems poised between two gazes, that of Scottie behind her (of whom she is supposedly unaware) and the intently focused gaze of Carlotta in the portrait.

Cued by Elster, Scottie believes that Madeleine believes that she is being taken over, possessed, by the spirit of her dead great-grandmother, the Carlotta in the portrait. Scottie endeavors to convince Madeleine that such a loss of identity is impossible, but the implications of the plot indicate that he believes, or comes to believe, this supernatural influence might exist. Scottie's fascination with the story of Carlotta fuels his attraction to Madeleine, and his own obsession with the portrait expresses his growing erotic fixation with this

fantasy. Thus the portrait in *Vertigo*, although dealing with some of the same themes as *The Lodger* and *Rebecca*, actually reverses the role portraits play in the earlier films. Whereas the pictures of blonde women and the portrait-come-to-life engender something close to disgust in the lodger and Max, this portrait kindles Scottie's desire. The scene that parallels the anti-erotic reaction expressed by the male characters in the earlier film appears in *Vertigo* in an almost opposite context. When his friend Midge Wood (Barbara Bel

Geddes) displays her painted parody of *Portrait of Carlotta*, an exact duplicate—except for her own excessively familiar and bespectacled face replacing Carlotta's mysterious gaze—Scottie is not amused ("that's not funny"). He walks out on their dinner date, shaking his head, causing the collapse of Midge's erotic hopes.[9] Scottie needs the portrait as part of his erotic fantasy of Madeleine/Carlotta (hence the impossibility of the "happy ending" resolution found in *Rear Window* of integrating his lover into his fantasy—Scottie actually *does* desire a dead woman, and her death plays an essential part in the fantasy).

Likewise Hitchcock employs the *tableau vivant* in *Vertigo* in a very different manner than in *Rebecca*. Hitchcock portrays Scottie's descent into madness as an elaborate dream sequence, involving a variety of filmic manipulations of space and image and the use of animation. The bouquet from the portrait appears, but as a filmic cartoon that proceeds to unravel itself in an animated flurry of petals and transforming colors. Within this dream Carlotta's portrait also appears, not as a painting but precisely as a *tableau vivant*, an actress filmed in the precise pose and costume of the portrait. The ontological status of this image within the film's diegesis poses a fascinating paradox. Hitchcock does not simply show the painting again, but rather a "real" woman. But could we claim the dream portrays the subject of the painting, Carlotta herself? The resemblance is precise (one assumes the portrait Hitchcock commissioned for the film took this young actress, Joanne Genthon, as its model). Yet there is little sense that we are supposed to take her as a "real" person within the film's diegesis. She appears frozen in her pose, a living picture, not a living person, an image visualized from Scottie's memory of the portrait, imprinted on his consciousness. As such, the presence of the living woman in the Carlotta pose represents not only his memory of the portrait, but his belief in the power Carlotta exerts: the return of the dead and their dreadful effect on the living. Overwhelmed by this persistence of the image of the portrait—not its emergence from the frame (at one point in the dream the wraith of Carlotta appears framed by the window between Scottie and Elster), but its transformation from the painterly to the virtual—Scottie becomes psychotic.

Scottie recovers from his psychosis and moves to an apparently healthier neurotic obsession: his discovery of Judy and his attempt to recreate her in the image of Madeleine. The tragic ironies of this Pygmalion story have been well analyzed, and although it certainly involves acts of artistic cre-

ation—fashioning, rehearsing, and recreating—the emphasis of this process lies more on bringing something to life than on the baleful image of the portrait (contrast this to Hitchcock's most likely ultimate source for this part of the film, the novel *Bruges-la-Morte* by Belgian symbolist Georges Rodenbach and its operatic version *Die tote Stadt* by Erich Korngold, in which a portrait of the dead wife plays an essential role). Scottie has no portrait of Madeleine that rules his recreation of Judy. Instead he attempts to recapture a memory, recreate it, and reinhabit it. At the film's climax, Scottie recaptures his vanished love and recoups lost time as he embraces Judy, now clothed and coiffed as Madeleine, as their hotel-room present merges with the mission locale from the past where he last embraced Madeleine.[10]

But this apparent triumph of love and fantasy over loss is followed by Scottie's tragic discovery of the frame. Not only does the fatal portrait of Carlotta reappear, but it triggers Scottie's realization he has been duped, framed and manipulated within another man's plot. Seated before a mirror, after their ecstatic act of lovemaking, Judy prepares to go out to dinner with her lover, and, while chatting about where they will go, she performs the fatal act of putting on the necklace, the replica (or the original? does it matter at this point?) of Carlotta's necklace in the portrait. Within the logic of the story, this action betrays Judy's complicity in Elster's plot through her possession of, as Scottie later puts it, a sentimental souvenir of the murder that she assisted. She therefore reveals the dark truth about the past: its manufactured nature and her own complicity. Within the logic of images created by Hitchcock's control of their visual presentation, an even more sinister pattern asserts itself. Scottie, standing behind his beloved, helps Judy with the clasp of the necklace. It is therefore as an image, a reflection in the mirror, that he first sees the fatal necklace. Hitchcock's camera moves in on the reflected necklace, then cuts to a camera movement back from the portrait, a movement that pulls back from a close-up view of the painted necklace until we see the scene of Judy seated before the portrait in the Gallery of the Legion of

Honor. Reflection and painting, past and present merge here—but lack the ecstatic eroticism of the previous embrace. The camera movements in and out on the images of the necklace certainly don't indicate a movement through space. Rather, camera movement evokes the force of the portrait, its seeming reentrance into the space of the characters. One can certainly see the extended dolly-out revelation of the portrait as a visualization of Scottie's memory, as he mentally compares the two necklaces. But the force of the camera movement signals not only the essential pivot of the plot of the film but the reemergence of the power of Carlotta, of the fatal portrait itself (it reverses the absorption of the camera into the details of the painting in the earlier scene). If the spinning, ecstatic camera movement during the embrace in the previous scene in the hotel room captures Scottie's triumph over time and loss, here the past reasserts its fatal claim, and the reemergence of the portrait (coming in effect from the depths of the mirror) announces the imminent death of Judy and of Scottie's love.

## Turn it to the Wall: Paintings as Indices of Guilt

These uncanny portraits of women all invoke the vengeful triumph of *Thanatos* over *Eros*. In the case of *Vertigo*, it is not only an obsession with a lost love but the guilt over a past act of murder and deception that emerges with the portrait's return. *Vertigo* represents the climax of Hitchcock's erotic and deadly portraits of women. In Hitchcock's cinema, however, the portrait as sign of guilt does not always carry an (overtly, at least) erotic charge, or produce an obsessive relation of imitation, or have quite so deadly results. Some portraits function fairly simply as images of superegos, virtual parental presences, and these can be male as well as female. *Suspicion* (1942) introduces the military portrait of Lina's father, left to his daughter and her husband in his will, clearly with the intention of maintaining a sense of presence in his daughter's life, keeping an eye (even if a painted one) on them. Both Lina (Joan Fontaine) and Johnnie (Cary Grant) address the portrait at separate moments in

the film; Lina at one point denies Johnnie's guilt as she speaks to it. Similarly, in *Psycho* (1960), Sam (John Gavin) asks Marion (Janet Leigh) whether, after the family dinner she has proposed to him as a way to meet respectably, they can send her sister to the movies and "turn mama's picture to the wall?" Marion reacts to this query with a surprising amount of alarm for a girl in a cheap hotel room meeting with her lover and dressed only in a bra and slip. Like the paintings of the girls in *The Lodger*, Hitchcock uses these portraits to embody the lingering impressions that the parents leave on their offspring.

The opposite cathexis of a parental portrait comes in the delightful scene in *Strangers on a Train* (1951) when Bruno (Robert Walker) reacts to the expressionistic painting his mother (Marion Lorne) has completed of a rather demonic St. Francis by bursting into delighted laughter and claiming, "That's him! That's Father!" Bruno scampers with joy at this simultaneously devilish and absurd portrait, believing he has abolished paternal authority with his plot to have his father killed. A reversal of Bruno's demonic rebellion before a parental portrait appears with the epiphanic climax of *The Wrong Man* (1956), as Manny Balestrero (Henry Fonda), falsely accused of robbery, prays humbly before an image of Christ. The shot-counter-shot between his beseeching gaze and the religious image eventually leads to a nearly supernatural dissolve between Fonda's face and the face of the actual thief (Richard Robbins), as if the all-seeing gaze of the Christ sought out and revealed this elusive villain to the camera.

But the most focused treatment of a painting as an indication of guilt comes rather early in Hitchcock's career, with the painting of the jester in his first sound film, *Blackmail*.[11] Other than *The Trouble with Harry* (1955), *Blackmail* is the only Hitchcock film in which a painter plays a major character, in this case Mr. Crewe, the would-be rapist and later victim (Cyril Ritchard). The scene that culminates in the killing in *Blackmail* already reveals Hitchcock as a mature storyteller, able to manipulate audience point of view in order to build a complex logic of imagery. In her trip upstairs to the wonderland of the artist's studio, Alice (Anny Ondra) is thrilled with the excitement and possible danger inherent in flaunting the rules of proper behavior for young girls. While the teasing games the young couple play with each other are certainly erotic, they also project the possibility of the artist creating a new identity for Alice, revealing her curiosity about a life outside her ordinary routine as a shopkeeping family's daughter and a policeman's girlfriend. As Alice looks around this strange yet inviting space, she crosses to the window and glances out. The point-of-view shot that follows shows a policeman down on the street passing through the glow of a street lamp. Alice's smile in the reaction shot that follows may indicate that the nearness of the law reassures her, or, alternatively, that she feels herself at this point to be above the law. She then glances off-screen to the left and seems more concerned by something she sees within the studio. Hitchcock cuts to a medium close-up of the face of a jester, contorted grotesquely and pointing his finger towards her. In this close framing, in which the limits of the canvas are not shown, the shot seems to reveal another person in the room. But Hitchcock's camera quickly pulls back, revealing that the face belongs to a painting on an easel, an academic image of a Rigoletto-like fool with cap and bells who is pointing out of the frame and apparently roaring with laughter. Alice giggles with delight (and perhaps relief) as she proclaims, "I say, *that's* good, isn't it?"

This introduction of the painting of the jester sets up the ambiguous relation between the space of a painting and the space of the viewer that Hitchcock will continue to develop in his later films. First, the jester's dominating gesture (is the pun here intentional on Hitchcock's part?) sweeps out of the frame even more strongly than the concentrated gaze in the gothic portraits. The pointing arm and finger deliver a phallic force to the jester's jovial, if not mocking, gaze. This truly is a painting that directly addresses its viewer aggressively. It seems to greet Alice's naive appearance in this bachelor flat with a vulgar and slightly sinister "The joke's on you!" But if the painting's message

is minatory, Alice doesn't get it—yet. Instead, her encounter with the painting sparks another Hitchcockian doubling of viewer and image. Alice's appreciation of it is accompanied by her own broad pointing gesture, her arm also upraised, as if the painting infected her with an impulse towards unconscious mimicry. Hitchcock intercuts the two pointing poses: they are not quite subject and portrait, but the visual doubling creates a sense of mirror and reflection, the image on the canvas seeming to have exerted an uncanny influence on the space outside.

After invoking the ambiguities of picturing, reference, and representation, Hitchcock provides, like the song in *Rear Window*, another tracing of the stages of the artistic process, beginning at the beginning: the blank canvas. Alice stands before a full-length canvas (which is propped on an easel) and strikes a pose, this time imitating an artist with palette and brush in hand, one of several role-playing games she performs in the studio. However, she holds the brush awkwardly and accidentally leaves a blot on the canvas. (In black and white this blot appears as a dark black spot, but one wonders if a color was intended. Given the nature of stains in Hitchcock—think of *Stage Fright* [1950] and *Marnie* [1964] most especially—one suspects the blot would have been red. But black, with its polar contrast with Alice's last name, "White," works very well, too.) Alice reacts to disfiguring the blank canvas with childlike alarm ("ooo—look what I've done!"—perhaps calling for attention as much as apologizing), and the artist expresses mock anger. He proposes to cover the blot by incorporating it into an image, telling Alice to "draw something." Alice first daubs an extremely childish face of a girl, a sort of "Self-Portrait of the Artist as a Five-Year-Old." She seems rather proud of her production but laughs when the artist pronounces it "rotten." He then proceeds to give Alice an up-close and personal lesson in drawing, attempting to make something out of "this masterpiece," continuing the process of covering a botched job with a more encompassing figure. Guiding her hand as a clear excuse for physical intimacy and control, Crewe causes the brush Alice holds to trace a body below the grotesque head she drew. If the head recalls a child's drawing and expression, the lithe form the artist makes Alice limn is clearly a sexually mature female nude. Alice blushes at her complicity in this image and stammers, "Oh, you *are* awful!" The total image is awful as well, a composite of overt childlike primitivism and muted academic eroticism (with its pronounced mismatch between head and body, the canvas anticipates Midge's mocking self-portrait as Carlotta). However, in spite of her supposed embarrassment, Alice decides she should sign the collaboration. As awkward as a schoolgirl wielding a too-large pencil, she prints out her name, "Alice White," beneath this semi-self-portrait.

Her attempted rape by Crewe that follows (and Alice killing him in self-defense) remains hidden behind a curtain drawn around the bed. When Alice emerges, clad only in her underwear, she shivers with the cold of the studio and the horror of what has just happened. Searching out the dress the artist had tossed away from her, she finds it draped over an easel. Removing the dress, Alice uncovers the painting of the jester, with his outstretched finger. Hitchcock shoots Alice staring directly into the camera as she confronts this image. She reaches out in anger and tears the canvas with her fingernails (the camera angle makes it almost appear as if she were attempting to tear at the screen itself). Alice now takes the painting's gesture as a leering accusation (and, one could add, an image of phallic violence pointed in her direction, a sort of visual rape). This direct interaction with Alice's situation creates one of the strongest instances in Hitchcock's cinema of the subject of a painting seeming to emerge from its frame and affect the viewer's world. Alice perceives the painting as a threat. In defiance and anger she tears at the image as if it had a life of its own. The torn canvas, with its gaping hole, denies the lively appearance of the painting. But its merely material nature does not prevent the painting from exerting its force into the world of the film, both when seized as evidence by the police and as a continued image of Alice's memory of the act.

Tearing the canvas, attempting to eradicate its image, expresses both Alice's rage and her feelings of guilt. Morally, of course, she is guilty only of an act of self-defense, and the guilt Hitchcock portrays remains a psychological effect of a patriarchal culture. It combines guilt over the killing with guilt over sexual temptation and possibly even loss of virginity (the advertising sign "White for Purity" that haunts Alice as she makes her way home through the London streets seems to indicate this). The ancient image of guilt as a stain or blot gives retroactive meaning to the daubed "self-portrait" that attempted to hide the original and accidental blot made by Alice's brushstroke.[12] Before she leaves the scene of the crime, she realizes she has left her name behind. She covers over her "signature" of the self-portrait with an emphatic brushstroke, making her name into an even larger blot than the one the painting was meant to refigure. The blotting out of her name removes essential evidence, of course, but also blots out her earlier childlike, innocent identity as "Alice White," now, within the system of patriarchy, reduced to a dark smudge.

Alice subsequently endures guilt, anxiety, and suspense over the discovery of the killing and the men who learn of her complicity (her policeman boyfriend and the eponymous blackmailer). Ultimately she makes a decision to confess to the police, an act interrupted by the death of her blackmailer and the intervention of her boyfriend. The apparent happy ending of Alice's deliverance from lawful punishment (and presumed social ostracism) is undercut brutally by the film's final images and sound. After being ignored by the police despite her desire to confess, Alice has her attempted confession silenced by her boyfriend. As she leaves police headquarters, an officer on duty mocks the possibility of her knowledge, asking if she was going to reveal the murderer. He jokes that soon they will be hiring "lady detectives." His laughter at his sexist remark fills the soundtrack, and Alice at first seems to join him with a relieved smile. However, she looks off-screen and sees the jester painting being carried down the corridor. Repeating its introduction in the studio, the camera initially frames the painting so that its edges are not visible and the jester for a moment seems alive. But the policeman carrying the canvas soon moves away from the camera, revealing the painting as a simple material object (and revealing the "self-portrait" being carried away as well). The framing of the jester, with his wide grin and his still-pointing finger, and especially the soundtrack of the policeman's laughter heard over the image, provide this painting with an uncanny life and a voice. Guilt seems inescapable, even for this reunited sympathetic couple, in one of Hitchcock's strongest images of a painting exerting a force beyond its edges.

## The Other Space: New Perspectives for Hitchcock

In many ways this essay is inspired by one of the foundational essays of 1970s film studies, Stephen Heath's "Narrative Space," which begins with a discussion of two very different paintings in Hitchcock's *Suspicion*.[13] The first is the portrait of Lina's father, discussed in the previous section, which Heath succinctly claims "bears with it all its Oedipal weight on the whole action of the film—the woman held under the eye of the father...."[14] In contrast to this "massive portrait" so firmly anchored in the symbolic system of the film and congruent not only with its narrative structure but with the spatial logic of looks and reactions that structure the relations of suspicion and guilt between the characters, Heath notes a different painting whose role is less certain. Two detectives visit Lina to question her about the death of Johnnie's companion, and their visit deepens her growing doubts about her husband's behavior. Benson (Vernon Downing), the younger detective (who, as Heath notes, plays little role in the questioning), encounters a different sort of painting (most likely a print) hanging in Lina's hallway. Heath underscores the lack of narrative purpose to this brief encounter, which is repeated: the detective reacts strangely to the picture, both as he comes in and as he leaves Lina's apartment. According to Heath, this reaction pulls the viewer "out of the action,

breaking the clarity of direction" as Benson's gaze itself is "pulled to the left."[15] The print is a cubistic still life vaguely reminiscent of Pablo Picasso's synthetic cubist period. The detective looks at it with incomprehension (Heath describes it as "fascinated panic"[16]—perhaps a somewhat melodramatic description, but not entirely off the mark). His reaction is underscored not only by the scene's repetition but by an unusual, atonal piano phrase on the soundtrack.

Hitchcock's orchestration of the looks surrounding the second painting is, in Heath's mind, a countermeasure to the clear regulation of narrative, significance, the rule of law, and the construction of narrative space that constitute a Hollywood film like *Suspicion*. This cubist print supplies no narrative clue, has no clear symbolic significance. Outside this scene it is never returned to. From this point of view the picture is "useless." Its modernist space, which presumably provokes the detective's "panic," poses a possible threat to the traditional construction of story, space, and perspective. The picture, as Heath puts it, prompts a "disbalance of the law and its inspecting eye," opening up, if briefly, "another scene, another story, another space."[17] One could accuse Heath of making much ado about nothing (one thinks of the trailer for *Psycho*, where Hitchcock, walking through the film's set, points at a picture on the wall and says with ironic humor, "This picture has *great* significance"). But that is Heath's point. The sequence is negligible narratively speaking—but then why is it there?

Two answers suggest themselves immediately. First, its presence has to be justified only if one thinks of narrative in film as a system that demands significance or some function for every element, or at least those elements that are given some saliency (as this one is through its repetition and its underlining on the soundtrack). But, in fact, I would argue against viewing Hollywood cinema as a classical system ruled exclusively by narrative coherence and economy. Instead I would maintain that Hollywood movies took as their model less the well-made play than the theatrical melodrama —a form overloaded with various attractions, in hopes that narrative patterns would corral it, or at least most of it, into some manageable form for viewers. In contrast to the Jamesian narrative tradition, Hollywood films aspired to be loose and baggy monsters. Thus, like their 19th century models, they are filled with lots of "useless" stuff, moments of spectacle, musical numbers, attractive stars, and especially bits of comic business—all of which can even be deleterious to a classical conception of narrative as a carefully determined economy of cause and effect and resolution. Thus Benson's reaction provides a bit of comic relief, an example of the humor that Hitchcock was known to pepper throughout his films, often poking fun at the police. I would maintain that most Hollywood features do not display a narrative economy that uses up all of its elements by describing the environment, advancing the action, defining characters, or creating symbolic structures (to cover Roland Barthes's main categories of narrative prose in *S/Z*). However... Alfred Hitchcock actually *did* seem to construct his films in an obsessive manner, so that it is possible to find cogent significance for most of his details (like the seemingly ambient sounds in *Rear Window*). This partly explains the critical industry that has grown up around his films, which constantly reward interpretation and analysis.

Another obvious explanation for the scene would see it as a typical Hollywood joke about modern art, a smack at elitist taste sure to get a guffaw from the yokels (my favorite example comes in the lecture on surrealism by the "hardboiled" museum curator played by Pat O'Brien in *Crack-up* [1946]—a tradition that continues at least until the insult delivered by the Drill Master in Stanley Kubrick's *Full Metal Jacket* [1987]: "You're so ugly you could be a masterpiece of modern art!"). But does Hitchcock consistently show this attitude toward modern painting? Curiously, a similar reaction to a work of modern art occurs in *Rear Window* when detective Tom Doyle (brought to Jefferies's apartment to hear his suspicions of Thorwald), eyes with confusion and possible distain a print of an Henri Matisse still life Jefferies has on the wall.[18] His reaction is not stressed as

strongly as Benson's in *Suspicion* (and the lack of a conventional score forbids a piano motif underscoring it). But perhaps proving Heath's point about the oddness of Benson's reaction, Doyle is a major character in the film, and his reaction accords with his pedestrian, prosaic lack of imagination or fancy.

Did Hitchcock share the typically negative attitudes towards modern and abstract art displayed by his detective characters? Such paintings subvert or avoid the perspectival system so essential for the effects of Hitchcock's paintings discussed so far, which depend on the creation of depth effects and a sense of illusionist representation. In this sense modern paintings open up a different scene, another space and perhaps another story. The incomprehension displayed by detectives Benson and Doyle becomes more clearly the sign of a narrow and even nasty view of the world in the sardonic comments Deputy Sheriff Calvin Wiggs (Royal Dano) makes about the abstract expressionist canvas painted by leading man Sam Marlowe (John Forsythe) in the only Hitchcock film in which abstract art plays an important role— the unfairly neglected and delightful *The Trouble with Harry*. *The Trouble with Harry* represents not only Hitchcock's most masterful comedy but his unique creation of a pastoral romance. By the end of the film Marlowe, the modern artist, becomes the center of a newly formed Dickensian community set in a bucolic New England. Hitchcock bases this ideal society in the victory of *Eros* over *Thanatos*, symbolized by the burying of the dead and the inauguration of new marriages among young and old alike, along with the recognition of the relativity of time ("tomorrow is yesterday") and the endless possibility of refashioning narrative explanations—even starting the action of the film over again at the ending.

As the narrow-minded maintainer of law and order, Wiggs plays a negative role and only overcomes his contempt for Marlowe's modern art when he believes it can be used as evidence of a crime. Sam's sketch of Harry's corpse is seized upon by Calvin as proof that a dead body did exist in the forest (a fact the main characters wish-

Sam Marlowe (John Forsythe) and Deputy Sheriff Calvin Wiggs (Royal Dano) with one of Marlowe's paintings of Harry in *The Trouble with Harry* (1955). Still courtesy of the Academy of Motion Picture Arts and Sciences. Rights courtesy of Universal Studios Licensing LLLP.

to conceal because each of them, other than Sam, fears she or he may be guilty of killing Harry). In this film, in a comic inversion of the usual Hitchcock plot, all trace of guilt evaporates when it is revealed that Harry died of natural causes. This comic denouement is anticipated stylistically when, before Calvin's outraged eyes, Sam reworks his drawing of Harry, changing his features and opening his eyes in order to demonstrate before the outraged representative of the law that art is based in the freedom of the imagination. Here, uniquely among his works, Hitchcock celebrates a zone of liberty within representation, an alternative role for art aside from an index of guilt or image of obsession. It is as though Midge's joke portrait succeeded in dissolving Carlotta's spell. In *The Trouble with Harry* the dead stay dead, no matter how often they are taken from the grave.

Is Benson's reaction, then, simply a joke, a ludic interlude, an invocation of another tone that Hitchcock will include briefly in his other films and develop fully only in *The Trouble with Harry* (and the humorous interludes in his television shows)? But rather than demonstrating its insignificance, this analysis perhaps shows that something very serious is at stake, a sort of reverse side to Hitchcock's concern with pictures and their limits. Hitchcock's playful nature often involves countermeasures within his significant structures, an impulse that, as Heath describes Benson's gaze, pulls us to the edge, out of the picture, hinting at another scene, another space. Like Edgar Allan Poe, to whom he is often compared (though usually with little thought about what the comparison would mean), Hitchcock knows that significance can hide itself in plain sight, or perhaps better put, plain sight can be a form of hiding. Thus his own seemingly joking gesture of pointing at the picture in the trailer to *Psycho* should, at second glance, make us seriously consider its significance. If *The Trouble with Harry*, with its bright Technicolor images of a New England fall and its shaggy dog story of a corpse unable to rest in its grave, presents Hitchcock's sardonic comedy of death and remarriage, then *Psycho* could be seen as its nega-

tive image, its flip side—Hitchcock's ultimate meditation on the sinister influence of the dead on the living, stripped even of the romanticism of *Vertigo*. A painting in *Psycho* literally reveals its underside and thereby leads us into another space.

Hitchcock's comment in the *Psycho* trailer (like many of his teasing, slightly misleading comments in this preview, hinting at the plot of the upcoming film he is announcing without really explaining it) about the "great significance" of the picture can be affirmed on two levels: first, the painting *does* play a role in the plot; second, the subject of the painting itself has symbolic significance. Let's take the symbolic reference first. While I don't believe anyone has identified it specifically (it is not any of the most famous treatments of the theme), the picture clearly portrays the biblical tale of Susannah and the Elders, as two elderly men struggle over a voluptuous female nude. An incident from the Old Testament (actually from the apocryphal 13th chapter of the Book of Daniel included in the Vulgate), the story concerns a pair of church elders who spy the lovely Susannah at her bath, attempt to force her to have sex, and, when she refuses, falsely accuse her of adultery. A primary text in sermons on hypocrisy and bearing false witness, the theme also provided a religious alibi for painting the nude in the 16th through the 18th centuries (including treatments by Jacopo Tintoretto, Rembrandt van Rijn, Artimesia Gentileschi, and Peter Paul Rubens), when painting nudity still could be considered scandalous.

The congruence between the painting's subject and the use Norman Bates (Anthony Perkins) puts it to is so exact, it strikes one as a Hitchcockian joke (an instance of the black humor that haunts the film and makes one recall Hitchcock's enigmatic claim that he considered *Psycho* a comedy). After Marion Crane leaves Norman's parlor (where the painting hangs) to go to her motel room next door, Norman crosses to the painting. Framed in medium shot, he removes it from the wall, uncovering a large, uneven circular indentation in the plaster revealing another surface, presumably the wall of Marion's adjoining room. In the center of this large opening, a small hole draws our attention through its bright illumination. Hitchcock cuts to a new angle, shooting Norman from the side and a bit closer. The light streaming through the small hole hits his face as he leans towards it. The next shot reveals Norman's point of view of Marion in her room undressing, the uneven border from the hole in the wall softly framing the view. Cutting at the moment when it seems Marion is about to remove her underwear, Hitchcock shows an extreme close-up of Norman's eye peering through the hole (whose uneven torn edge is visible to the right), shot from the side, showing the beam of light from the hole brightly illuminating his eye as it shifts, watching intently. Hitchcock returns us to Norman's point of view, showing Marion pulling a robe about her before she exits from the frame. The instant of nakedness has been replaced by the almost clinical enlargement of the eyeball, almost pierced by a probing point of light. The nearly physical impact of voyeurism as an interplay of orifices and light has never been so brilliantly exposed.

Commentators have noted that Norman's voyeuristic entertainment recalls the cinema, the light coming from the peephole figuring the projector beam and Norman's position in the darkness of the parlor watching the bright spectacle of Marion's nudity recalling the archetypal cinema viewer (e.g., André Bazin's description of the moviegoer as a voyeur looking through a keyhole, in contrast to a member of the more communal audience at the theater).[19] I would agree with this, and relate it (as one could detail in another essay) to the many invocations of cinema projection in Hitchcock, most of them more literal (the complex play with the films shown in the cinema in *Sabotage* [1936], the film showing in *Saboteur* [1942], and, of course, the invocation of cinema spectatorship so often analyzed in *Rear Window*). There is no question that Hitchcock uses a system of references in his films to refer self-consciously to cinema spectatorship, including not only paintings but photographs, theatrical prosceniums, windows, costumes, performances, and arrangements of light.

Norman Bates (Anthony Perkins) in a promotional photograph for *Psycho* (1960). Rights courtesy of Universal Studios Licensing LLLP.

But within my more limited focus in this essay on pictures and their edges and frames, I want to linger over the fact that Hitchcock conceals this private cinema *behind* a framed picture.

Although the picture hides something, the image actually displays what it hides: a scenography of voyeurism. As I indicated in the previous sections, the portraits of the dead and the pictures serving as indices of guilt seem to exceed their frames, projecting a baleful influence, a process often visualized by camera movement both towards the painting (eliminating the frame from view) and back out (revealing the frame or edge, but often also expressing the force of their gaze or influence). In this sequence Hitchcock seems to turn his schema around, revealing the underside of representation. The projective power lies behind the painting, and its ultimate sources lie literally in another space, another scene, the room next door. Rather than the force of guilt, it is the glaring illumination of the object of desire, which the screen cannot show directly, that projects itself into the eye of the beholder. After viewing this scene, Norman replaces the picture over its aperture. In medium shot we see him, his face half marked by shadow as his mouth compresses and his eyes stare intently. We know from the subsequent actions that his vision has not only excited his lust but also his guilt and impulse towards punishment, triggering the murder of Marion, punishing her for a sexual titillation entirely due to Norman's own voyeurism (like the plot of the Elders against Susannah). Thus guilt and violence of the sort depicted in the painting serve as a screen to block and transform the image of desire, a visual filter that darkens and perverts the sexual impulse.

In his note for the all-too-famous shower scene (to which this act of voyeurism serves as prelude), Hitchcock described the knife thrusts as seeming to tear at the screen.[20] This fascinating comment makes one reflect that violence in Hitchcock often seems to emerge from the screen, to target the viewer. The figure of the painting emerging from its frame fits into a larger Hitchcockian picture. As anchored as his space seems in its subservience

to narrative, as centered and orderly as his compositions are, I would maintain, they reoccurringly open onto another space, onto energies that remain beyond the grasp of the visual and beyond the limits of the frame. If their source remains by necessity unnameable and beyond the configuration of the visual, nonetheless we can locate their destination in the reverse angle from the screen, in the eye of the viewer who receives the projected and reflected beam of light.

## Epilogue: Hitchcock in the Art of Others

While Hitchcock can, and has been, understood as the master of framing, the visual storyteller who above all knows how to make an image tell a story, how to make it bear meaning and narrative trajectory, we must acknowledge that this mastery is founded upon a deep suspicion of the lure of the picture, the trap that framing can imply. Behind his reveling in visual expression lies an abyss not only of violence but of the nothingness on which both desire and the image are founded and founder. I know of no more eloquent expression of this aspect of Hitchcock's work than comments in an essay by the contemporary artist Robert Morris in which he speaks of the influence of Hitchcock, and *Vertigo* specifically, on his own work from the 1969 *Finch College Project*. This work, which deals with the surfaces of the image as both reflection and depiction, its construction and disassembly, could hardly seem further from a Hitchcock film. And yet they share, according to Morris (and I think it is a profound insight), what he describes as his work's "iconoclastic and iconophobic tenor."[21] While Morris's own fascination with visual erasure may seem part of a minimalist strategy of the late 1960s art world, his own discussion invokes Hitchcock's "ability to at once deflate and promote the image, achieving a kind of simultaneous cancellation and elevation."[22] Although Morris does not specifically cite the uses of painting in *Vertigo*, he indicates, "I was impressed with how Hitchcock loads and manipulates the image to create an illusory, irrational, delusional, and nauseating space. Always threatening in this film is that irrational, delusional, and nauseating space that overpowers linguistic rationality."[23] We could see the frame in Hitchcock not only as an attempt to direct the viewer's attention, but as an attempt at containment of threatening forces—a containment that his stories more often undermine than sustain. Something emerges from Hitchcock's frames, as something lies behind them. What? Perhaps what the painting in *Psycho* shows us is that behind the framed depiction lies the nothingness of infinite regress, the spirals of desire and the violence born of emptiness.

I have primarily treated the frame in this essay as the periphery of a picture that defines its ontological separation from the world of the observer, even if, as we have seen, Hitchcock ultimately questions the possibility of such a separation. But in his play between the fixity of the image and the motion that characterizes both the cinema and the phenomenal world, we can conceive of another sort of frame essential to the cinematographic illusion: the individual frames of film, projected in the sound era 24 times a second. In contrast to Hitchcock's display of the frame of paintings and the unique role they play within his oeuvre, the individual film frames remain invisible, an implicit technology rather than an aesthetic tool, shared by all makers of cinema, the basis of its representation of motion.[24] But perhaps the most famous and successful appropriation of Hitchcock by the contemporary art world (as opposed to his own appropriation of images of modern art), Douglas Gordon's *24 Hour Psycho* (1993), undertakes to display precisely the individual frames that underlie one of Hitchcock's greatest works. This transformation of the narrative drive of *Psycho* into a stuttering barely moving exercise in duration can be seen as another in the long (exhausted?) tradition of modernist works undoing the illusions of traditional works, alienating a viewer from their fascination and revealing their material substrate. More interesting, however, is Laura Mulvey's claim that this work is "a celebration of the new radical possibilities offered by video viewing."[25] Although Mulvey (somewhat too hastily, I think) sees the work as an elegy for the death of cinema, I believe instead it reveals the inexhaustible nature of the cinematic image, its negotiations, within fragments of seconds, of the acts of narration, representation— and of their critique. Perhaps most revealing, Gordon has indicated that the piece occurred to him when he happened to watch a sequence of *Psycho* in frame-by-frame mode. What sequence? Norman Bates removing the painting of Susannah and the Elders and looking through the peephole at Marion. Gordon's dark transformation of Hitchcock springs, I would claim, from that discovery of the underside of representation: the interval between picture, image, and eye focused within the aggressive probe of light piercing the darkness, that slow, constant, and invisible series of eclipses triggered by the revolving shutter hiding and revealing the individual frames that make the illusion of cinema possible.

# 4

# *I Confess* and *Nos deux consciences*

BILL KROHN

The following half-page ad appeared in issue number 72 of *Cahiers du cinéma* on the occasion of the French release of *The Wrong Man* in 1957: "The *Cahiers du cinéma* thank ALFRED HITCHCOCK, who has just made 'The Wrong Man' solely to give us pleasure and show the world to its face the Truth of our exegeses."[1]

American critics by and large disapproved of *The Wrong Man* as a deviation from Hitchcock's role as artful entertainer, the Master of Suspense, but for his French exegetes the true story of an innocent man whose life is devastated when he is falsely accused of a series of holdups was a powerful expression of the theme they believed gave depth to even the lightest Hitchcock entertainments: the transference of guilt.

This idea was first advanced in an article about *Under Capricorn* (1949) in *La Gazette du cinéma* by Jacques Rivette, who would become the leading theorist of the *Cahiers* group. Even more detested by American critics than *The Wrong Man*, *Under Capricorn* harked back to Hitchcock's youthful interest in melodrama, movingly embodied in another commercial failure, *The Manxman* (1929), which was also much admired in France.[2]

In fact, it appears that *Under Capricorn* was the film that clinched Hitchcock's French reputation. Filmmaker-critic Alexandre Astruc (one of the edi-

tors of *Gazette du cinema*) helped launch the *Cahiers* with an article in the first issue defending this period drama as superior even to *Stromboli* (1950)—a sublime film by Roberto Rossellini built around the same actress, Ingrid Bergman. "Like Maurice Scherer, I would give all of *Stromboli*," Astruc wrote, "for the one shot in *Under Capricorn* where a woman's face is suddenly more vast than the sea."[3]

Maurice Scherer was the pen name of another filmmaker-critic who would become famous as Eric Rohmer. Three years later, in an article about cinematic modernism, he proposed as the summit of modernism *I Confess* (1953), a drama about transference of guilt enacted in the archetypal context of the Roman Catholic confessional.[4]

*Under Capricorn, I Confess,* and *The Wrong Man*—all viewed as aberrations in the United States—were the key films in Hitchcock's work as analyzed by Rohmer and his colleague Claude Chabrol in their 1957 book *Hitchcock*, which concludes with *The Wrong Man* as the QED of the authors' demonstration. "Our commentary on this film, which casts a singular illumination on the preceding works," they wrote, "can take the place of a concluding recapitulation."

Along with the very effective thriller *Strangers on a Train* (1951), these unfashionable melodramas are the Hitchcock films in which the transference of guilt theme is developed most overtly.

*Under Capricorn*: Hattie Flusky (Ingrid Bergman) killed her own brother to keep him from shooting her husband Sam (Joseph Cotten). Sam assumed her crime and paid the penalty of transportation to Australia. Hattie's guilt drives her to drink and almost to her death before her confession, filmed in a ten-minute take, "delivers her from memory by giving it a verbal body… the confession of sins is the equivalent of their redemption."

*I Confess*: Father Michael Logan (Montgomery Clift) is accused of a murder committed by his sacristan, Otto Keller (O. E. Hasse), who confessed his sin to the priest right after committing it. Only the real murderer's confession can establish Logan's innocence, while saving the soul of the man he cannot denounce because his knowledge of the crime was obtained in the confessional.

*Strangers on a Train*: Tennis pro Guy Haines (Farley Granger) has a chance encounter with wealthy psychotic Bruno Anthony (Robert Walker), who proposes a scheme for exchanging murders. When Guy demurs, Bruno murders Guy's estranged wife, then tries to blackmail him into fulfilling his part of the "bargain"—the murder of Bruno's hated father.

*The Wrong Man*: Manny Balestrero (Henry Fonda), a musician struggling to support his family, is wrongly accused of sticking up an insurance company and a liquor store. Jailed overnight, he is freed on bail and begins the torturous process of trying to clear himself. Halfway through the film, his calvary becomes his wife's as she sinks into a clinical depression, convinced that what is happening to them is somehow her fault.

In *The Wrong Man* Hitchcock had already embarked upon a variation on a theme that Rohmer and Chabrol's colleague Jean-Luc Godard would describe as "a transfer of innocence,"[5] because neither Manny nor his wife is guilty of anything. Instead of a confession, the film ends with an exchange of looks between the real holdup man and Manny "by which the first passes the second the baton of his guilt."[6] "Transference of guilt" was not a blueprint for making films—variations played on the theme in Hitchcock's films were unceasingly inventive, like the oeuvre as a whole.

Before making *The Wrong Man*, Hitchcock had already treated the transference theme from the standpoint of psychoanalysis in *Spellbound* (1947) and with baroque exuberance in *The Trouble with Harry* (1955), where every character in the ensemble cast blithely assumes responsibility

for the film's original sin: murdering Harry. In the end it turns out that he died of a heart attack. And of course all of Hitchcock's "wrong man" entertainments, from *The 39 Steps* (1935) through *North by Northwest* (1959), turn thriller conventions into allegorical expressions of the transference theme.

But for the authors of *Hitchcock* it was evident that the theme was ingrained in Hitchcock by his Catholic upbringing, and this hypothesis finds its ideal confirmation in *I Confess*, the plot of which imitates the central archetype of Christian allegory, a symbolic system to which Western culture is still indebted. In *I Confess* transference of guilt is an *imitatio Christi*, embodied in the story of a priest accused of a crime committed by a man whose confession he has heard.

This is a solidly traditional allegorical reading of Hitchcock's film—or more properly, a figural one: a particular type of allegorical reading based on the theological concept of *figura*, by which Old Testament prefigures New and worldly things "figure" supernatural ones. To put it in more familiar language, Father Logan is a Christ figure.

The analogy was even more complete in a number of screenplay drafts written before Warner Bros. told Hitchcock that Father Logan could not be executed for a murder he didn't commit. Hitchcock would have preferred that Christ's vicar literally assume not only the guilt, but also the punishment, for another man's crime.

André Bazin, although he was not himself a "Hitchcocko-Hawksian," was therefore understandably surprised when the director told him in 1954 that *I Confess* was a failure because it lacked humor, evincing a preference for his English work in this regard. Feeling a responsibility to defend the point of view of his young Turks, Bazin was actually the first, in the course of the same interview, to explain the workings of the now-famous "transference" to Hitchcock:

"The translation of such a subtle argument was not easy. Hitchcock listened attentively and intensely. When he finally understood it, I saw for the first and only time during our interview that he had been touched by an idea he had not and could not have thought of himself. I had found the chink in his armor of humor. He smiled delightedly, and I could see the idea working its way through his mind. The more he thought about it, the more he saw with satisfaction how accurate it was, and it was he who went on to find further justification for the theory in the stories of *Rear Window* (1954) and *To Catch a Thief* (1955). This was the only victory I was able to achieve for Hitchcock's exegetes, but if the theme does indeed exist in his work, it is thanks to them that he has discovered it."[7]

This conversation occurred on the set of *To Catch a Thief*, in which a retired cat burglar (Cary Grant) has to come out of retirement to catch a "copycat" burglar (Brigitte Auber) in order to prove his own innocence. Even though it is one of Hitchcock's most lighthearted entertainments, *To Catch a Thief* is punctuated by sudden fades to nightshade green (the color of death in the Hitchcock rainbow), suggesting unsuspected depths that the film's sunny romantic adventure dances over.

But of course by then *Under Capricorn* had already given incandescent expression to the theme of transference in Bergman's ten-minute confession. Speaking of the influence *Under Capricorn* exerted on Hitchcock's subsequent films, Rohmer and Chabrol explained, "The more manifest profundity of this work would, so to speak, be splashed on all the others."[8]

The same thing could be said of *I Confess*, made five years later, just before two light entertainments to which it may have imparted a certain gravitas: *Dial M for Murder* (1954), in which the victim of an attempted murder is condemned to be executed for killing her attacker in self-defense, and *Rear Window*, in which a neighborhood voyeur is increasingly tainted with guilt for a murder he believes has been committed because he *wants* it to have happened.

Forewarned by Bazin's experience, François Truffaut would be careful during his marathon interview with Hitchcock not to overplay his hand with respect to *I Confess*, as Rivette had been in his *Cahiers* review of the film, where he explicitly avoided defending Hitchcock by "arguing the profundity and permanence of his subjects."[9] What the young Turks were in no position to consider at the time was the possibility that *I Confess* had played a revelatory role for Hitchcock himself, long before Bazin explained the workings of transference of guilt to him on the set of *To Catch a Thief*.

John Russell Taylor suggests as much in his biography *Hitch*, where we learn that Paul Anthelme's 1902 play *Nos deux consciences* had "haunted" the director since he saw a production of it sometime in the early 1930s. The play was first sold by the author's nephew to the playwright and literary agent Louis Verneuil, who sold it to Hitchcock in 1947 after very protracted negotiations.[10] Hired to write a treatment for a screen adaptation of *Our Two Consciences*, Verneuil would be the first of a long string of writers who worked on the screenplay of *I Confess*.

Themes and archetypes are among the ghostly baggage auteur criticism has inherited from its founders, at least one of whom, Rohmer, was a professed Platonist. What makes *I Confess* such an interesting subject for further research, apart from its considerable qualities as a film, is the possibility that Anthelme's play may have served as a material archetype—a template—for the first manifestations of the transference theme and its corollary, the theme of confession, in Hitchcock's 1930s thrillers, particularly *The Man Who Knew Too Much* (1934) and *The 39 Steps*.

To see the form in which the transference theme haunted him after discovering Anthelme's play, we need to turn to the play itself. That has been difficult for researchers to do, even in France, because *Nos deux consciences* is very difficult to find even there. Fortunately there is an English translation commissioned by Hitchcock in the Warner Bros. script archives for *I Confess*.

In a small French village Father Michel Pieux and his friend Bordier, a Socialist politician who is the priest's favorite verbal sparring partner, discuss Bordier's belief that religion is obsolete, replaced by socialism—Bordier offers this as an explanation for the hostility the men of the village have shown to Michel. After that, the story is fairly close to the film, but the murderer plays a less important role in it than the socialist friend.

It turns out that Bordier's wife had an affair with Father Pieux's brother Philippe, by whom she had a child. The brother is dead for unspecified reasons, and because Michel was seeing Bordier's wife about the boy when "old Fenaille," who had been blackmailing her, was killed, she can alibi him.

When Bordier learns of his wife's past affair, he is faced with a dilemma: if she goes to the magistrate to alibi Michel, Bordier will be dragged into a scandal and lose a tight election that is imminent. Although the socialist cause will be hurt, he does not hesitate. True to his friendship and his humanist ethics, he sends his wife to alibi Michel, but all this does is supply the police with their missing motive.

The priest is tried and condemned. Visited by the murderer in jail, he hears his confession but prevents him from confessing to the police—if the killer cleared him that way, Michel would have saved his own life by using the confessional to frighten him into confessing to the police, a mortal sin for a priest. Instead he orders him to make restitution of the money he stole from his victim. Only after Michel is executed does the killer, seeing the news posted on the prison door, cry out his confession to the mob that is there to watch.

If Hitchcock's religious training—he was, after all, educated by Jesuits—enabled him to recognize the figural meaning of Anthelme's drama when he saw it on stage, it is certainly easy to understand his stubbornness about filming this story, for which the development process dragged on over five years in the teeth of doubt by Warner Bros. and the defection of his producing partner, Sidney Bernstein. After all, it isn't every day one finds a realistic dramatic situation that so powerfully evokes the meanings and emotions of a Passion play. Even a successful Christ allegory like Frank Borzage's *Strange Cargo* (1940) needed supernatural elements to pull off the parallels.

## The Case of the Missing Confession

There are two phases in the development of the theme of transference of guilt in Hitchcock's English work. During the first the theme is expressed in the ironic form of scapegoat dramas: stories of innocents who become the repository for other people's guilt. It is only when the transference of guilt is put right by confession that the theme assumes its familiar form. As it happens, the dividing line between the two phases seems to coincide with the period when Hitchcock told Taylor he first encountered *Nos deux consciences*.

Before that, Hitchcock's Catholic upbringing merged with an early experience—buried among memories of early childhood, although it would be trotted out for inspection often enough in later years—to create an affinity for the theme of the scapegoat: the famous childhood trauma of being locked up in a jail cell at age five on orders from his father for a childish offense that scarcely called for such retribution.

Hitchcock slyly told both Taylor and Truffaut that he had been a very well-behaved child whose father referred to him as "my lamb without a spot"—an expression of paternal affection that is less reassuring if we remember that "the lamb without a spot" was a biblical epithet for Christ the sacrificial victim (John 17: 20, 1 Peter 1:19), prefigured in the Old Testament by the lamb that is substituted at the last minute for Isaac after God has ordered Abraham to sacrifice his son. The myth of the divine scapegoat had even found its way into Hitchcock's personal history, but the symbolic form he imparted to it came from texts like the *Agnus dei* that were drummed into him by the Catholic liturgy, to which his father's strange endearment consciously alluded.

As for the first appearance of the "wrong man" theme in a Hitchcock film, it was an assignment from his first producer. His second film, *The Mountain Eagle* (1926), has since been lost, but unlike the "Ur-Hamlet," its basic outline has been preserved. It was a melodrama of life in the Kentucky hills in which a village justice of the peace, Pettigrew, secretly lusts after a woman he suspects of seducing his crippled son. His attentions send her fleeing into the arms of a mysterious hermit, Fear o' God. Pettigrew accuses the solitary of murdering his son, who has disappeared. Fear o' God is imprisoned—the first unjust imprisonment in

the oeuvre—and escapes. After a violent confrontation with Pettigrew he is cleared when the son reappears.

Here we have, in the form of an old-fashioned melodrama (made on soundstages in Germany, with Pettigrew played by the actor who played Death in Fritz Lang's *Destiny*, the film that made Hitchcock want to make films), all the elements of the transference of guilt theme, with religious and Freudian elements in abundance to tie it to Hitchcock's personal history as an English Catholic whose father had rather original ideas about child rearing. And yet every biographical source tells us that *The Mountain Eagle* was a film Hitchcock made because he had no choice and later dismissed as awful.

This kind of thing happens so often in auteurist studies that it suggests a materialist hypothesis about where archetypes come from: they come from texts—texts that are almost always encountered by chance, particularly at the outset of a director's career. When a director films even an imposed scenario, the film that results is a reading of that text, and once that film has become part of the oeuvre it can be reread in its turn, each new reading being a new film.

So *The Mountain Eagle* is already part of the intertext of the film that followed it, which Hitchcock asked studio head Michael Balcon to let him make: *The Lodger* (1926). Based on a novel he had seen acted on stage, *The Lodger* was, he always said, the "first real Hitchcock film," meaning that he had a free hand making it except for a happy ending necessitated by the star system: the hero, accused of being a serial killer, is nearly lynched by an angry mob before the real killer is caught, a scene that evokes the crucifixion through the famous image of the hero dangling from a spiked fence in which his handcuffs have been snagged while the mob threatens to dismember him.

*The Lodger* is a reading not only of the best-selling novel on which it was based (in which the lodger really is the serial killer everyone suspects him of being) but of *The Mountain Eagle*. The happy ending, which makes it a better "fit" for the transference theme than a faithful adaptation would have been, was yet another studio imposition. To complicate things further, that happy ending was also inspired by the comic stage adaptation of *The Lodger* that Hitchcock had seen in his teens—as was, perhaps, the cuckoo clock that startles the lodger by going off when he first appears at the door.

Considerably knottier than the notion of a timeless idea descending from the heavens or rising up gradually from the depths, this model would also have to take into account another kind of reading involved in any creation: the misreading of sources posited by Harold Bloom in *The Anxiety of Influence*, where he elaborates the theory that the preferred strategy for poets seeking to overcome their anxiety about being influenced by their poetic forebears is to misread the threatening precursor's work. More than most Hitchcock films, *The Lodger* wears its influences on its sleeve—all of German Expressionism, which it parodies brilliantly.

It would appear that Balcon, the head of Gainsborough Studios—who encouraged Hitchcock to try his hand at directing, assigned him *The Mountain Eagle* as his second film, and let him make *The Lodger* as his third—knew his star director well. By way of contrast, from the standpoint of the evolution we are tracing, the first films Hitchcock made after leaving Gainsborough for British International Pictures (BIP) would be something of a detour. And it was when Hitchcock rejoined Balcon at another studio in the 1930s that he began making the kind of thrillers for which he would become famous.

While Hitchcock was still at Gainsborough, waiting to move to the better-financed BIP, stories of innocents falsely accused seemed to keep finding their way to him: *Downhill* (1927), in which an innocent youth is expelled from Oxford for supposedly impregnating a girl who was really his best friend's mistress (honor forbids him to speak in his own defense), and *Easy Virtue* (1927), based on a Noel Coward play about a woman whose reputation is ruined when her jealous husband attacks a boy he wrongly suspects of being her

lover. At the beginning of *Easy Virtue* Hitchcock created a courtroom sequence intercut with flashbacks—a brilliant film-within-the-film with no equivalent in Coward's play—that is a nightmare of maligned innocence, as wrenching in its own way as *The Wrong Man.*

After three films for BIP that won't concern us, Hitchcock made what he called his "last silent film." Based on a badly written novel that was thrust upon him by the prestige-minded studio heads at BIP, *The Manxman* fully deserves the praise heaped on it by Rohmer and Chabrol—which makes it all the more surprising that they do not cite it as an early instance of the transference theme.

*The Manxman* is a melodrama about a romantic triangle that reaches its climax when the protagonist, who has just become a judge, has to preside over the trial of the mother of his illegitimate child for attempting suicide after confessing her sin to her husband, without naming the real father. The one flashy effect in this sober film is a dissolve from the black waters swallowing her to the ink in which the judge, on his first day in court, dips his pen, establishing an ironic link between her desperate act and his new eminence.

But for the moment Hitchcock seems to have embraced the idea of transference as embodied in the figure of the scapegoat without understanding the symbolic link between transference and confession—in fact, he and his collaborator Eliot Stannard rewrote the ending of *The Manxman* to play down the judge's confession (ultimately inspired, one suspects, by *The Scarlet Letter*), perhaps because they feared it would strike audiences as implausible.

In the novel the judge confesses in open court, prodded only by his conscience; in the film the ruined girl's father intuits his guilt and publicly accuses him, provoking his confession. Acknowledging his sin, the judge removes his wig, steps down, and takes the girl's arm. In the last shot they are surrounded by village mockers as they march off into their future with their illegitimate child.

Confession—a tricky act to put across cinematically without provoking yawns or laughter, as Hitchcock was to discover in the 1940s—finally becomes an issue in *Blackmail* (1929), only to be avoided at the last minute. The heroine is prevented by her policeman boyfriend from confessing that she committed the murder for which a sinister blackmailer has been hounded to his death. She attempts to make a clean breast of it to the head of Scotland Yard in a suspenseful scene where the audience is meant to root for her to keep her mouth shut.

A providential phone call creates an opening for the boyfriend to intervene, but the last shot of a painted jester mocking the couple as they exit Scotland Yard reminds us that we have been rejoicing in the death of a scapegoat: the blackmailer was guilty, but not of murder. His fate echoes that of another shady-looking character we watch being arrested, booked, and incarcerated in the film's documentary-style prologue, which is filmed in a way that inclines us to sympathize with the presumed criminal—the second reenactment of Hitchcock's youthful run-in with the police.

In the play *Blackmail* was based on, the girl discovers at the last minute that she didn't kill anyone, but Hitchcock wanted to explore the darkest implications of the story by ending the film with the boyfriend booking the self-confessed murderess and locking her away, in a sequence that would have echoed the documentary-style prologue. In this case the studio's insistence on a happy ending prevented him from filming a confession that would have ended the film on a sour note not unlike the one on which it does end. However he chose to play out the story, at this point in Hitchcock's career the ironies implicit in the figure of the scapegoat could result only in tragedy or in grim derision—the tightrope on which the ending of *The Manxman* also teeters uncertainly.

*Murder!* (1930) and its German doppelgänger *Mary* (1931) return to the theme of the falsely accused innocent and resolve it through the efforts of a detective who also happens to be a director. The gravity of the opening scene of the murder being discovered, and of the trial, the jury deliberations, and the subsequent visit of the hero to the incarcerated heroine, is continually undercut by unfunny horseplay. The director-detective solves

the murder in the conventional way and uses ponderous scare tactics to drive the guilty party to commit suicide during his trapeze act, a flashy climax that is followed by the reading of the killer's written confession. That scene is a good example of the conventional utilitarian function of confessions in theater and film. The killer's suicide note explains past events and supplies a proof that saves an innocent woman from being executed, but it is devoid of dramatic interest and stops the film cold while it is being read.

## Enter *Nos deux consciences*

It was after this that Hitchcock must have encountered Paul Anthelme's *Our Two Consciences*, the text that enabled him to complete the personal myth that would shape many of his best films. It seems reasonable, in the absence of any listing of dates that would permit us to nail down a production that he could have seen, to take the phrase "sometime in the early '30s" as referring to some time before 1934, when Hitchcock made *The Man Who Knew Too Much*, an original story in which the full pattern appears for the first time, even if Rohmer and Chabrol save their analysis of it for the 1956 remake because in the 1934 version "the implications are timidly expressed, and the details stingily distributed."[11]

Nevertheless, all the elements are there: a woman hears a dying man's secret—an assassination plot—which she and her husband are obliged to keep quiet about because their child is being held hostage to ensure their silence, until the famous scene in Albert Hall where she screams just before the assassin fires, diverting his aim. In fact, the basic pattern is clearer in this version, where it is the woman who both hears the secret and "confesses" it when she screams.

This does not, of course, keep the 1956 version, where husband and wife are treated as two sides of one character, from being superior in every respect—in no small part because some of the profundity unveiled in *I Confess* in 1952 "splashed on" the remake, to use Rohmer and Chabrol's metaphor for what I call "reading," just as Hitchcock's first encounter with *Nos deux consciences* years earlier seems to have "splashed on" the 1934 version.

The first time a character freely confesses in a Hitchcock film, he does it for no reason at all and with no connection to the rest of the plot, in which an innocent man is pursued for murder while seeking the meaning of his supposed victim's dying words, "The 39 Steps." In Hitchcock's 1935 film of that name, loosely adapted from John Buchan's novel, the hero, just as the police are closing in on him, hurls the question at an artiste on a music hall stage, Mr. Memory: "What are the 39 Steps?"

Very improbably, Mr. Memory, who is part of the film's sinister conspiracy, answers that "the 39 Steps" is a spy ring that steals government secrets and sells them, provoking the head spy, who is in the audience, to shoot him. With the police listening and chorus girls dancing in the background, the dying Mr. Memory recites the stolen secret he was supposed to carry out of the country in his brain, averring that it is "a load off my mind" just before expiring. In the foreground the heroine takes the hero's hand, from which dangles the pair of handcuffs that bound them together when they were fugitives.

"In Mr. Memory's death Hitchcock displays and, in effect, demonstrates, the mechanism of confession...." write Rohmer and Chabrol. "This subordinate theme is not enough in itself to confer value on *The 39 Steps*, but it brings a precious stone to the construction of the Hitchcock universe, sketched in his earliest films. And it also reinforces all the more the work's astonishing formal qualities"[12]—qualities all the more astonishing because of the unmotivated arbitrariness of this sudden appearance of confession as a dramatic climax, linked to other motifs in a pattern that finally makes symbolic sense, even though from a realistic standpoint it makes no sense at all.

If the first two English thrillers announce the premises of the oeuvre to come, the last four show Hitchcock rereading himself, trying to understand retrospectively what he had intuitively produced in *The Man Who Knew Too Much* and *The 39 Steps*.

His next two spy thrillers were serious films based on W. Somerset Maugham's *Ashenden, the Secret Agent*, two episodes of which became *The Secret Agent* (1936), and Joseph Conrad's black comedy about anarchist terrorism, *The Secret Agent*, which became *Sabotage* (1936).

Innocents are again sacrificed in these films. The blundering agents in the first kill the wrong man, and the blundering terrorist in the second accidentally blows up his young stepson, along with a bus full of Londoners—an error Hitchcock told interviewers he would never repeat. He was speaking of the theory of suspense, but from the point of view of his evolving myth, these films are a regression to the ironic version of the theme of the scapegoat that we saw in *Blackmail*, which could now be carried to its logical conclusion thanks to the power accorded Hitchcock by the great success of his two previous thrillers.

Afterwards, for the last two English thrillers, he returns with *Young and Innocent* (1937) to the screwball comedy treatment of the "wrong man" in *The 39 Steps* and achieves perfection of another kind with *The Lady Vanishes* (1938), where his moral sense exercises its teeth on the general complicity with fascism that unites against hero and heroine, for a time, all the passengers on the train.

Even though *The Lady Vanishes* has always been one of Hitchcock's best-loved films, Rohmer was not fooled. (He and Chabrol actually quite disliked *Sabotage*.) Reviewing *The Lady Vanishes* when it was rereleased in France in 1952, he devoted at least as much space to Hitchcock's recent films, which he preferred for their thematic richness: "Who can deny," he writes, "that from *Rebecca* to *Strangers on a Train* Hitchcock has with an ever more advanced knowledge applied himself to this difficult design: that there is not one single look given by the actors he is directing that doesn't bear the trace of the trouble that *also* inhabits the others?"[13]

The arc from Hitchcock's first American film, made under the boot of David O. Selznick, to his first film as a producer-director for Warner Bros. culminates, according to Rohmer and Chabrol, in the revelations of *Under Capricorn*, *Strangers on* a Train, and I Confess. But Laurence Olivier's confession in Rebecca (1940) (based on a novel that Hitchcock had tried to buy, only to be outbid by his future employer) is already a satisfactory resolution of a transference of guilt plot that anticipates Under Capricorn, where Bergman's confession, far from being just a device for informing the audience about the past, "is considered as an end in itself, as a privileged, even extraordinary attitude."[14]

A missed step: the cancelled ending of Suspicion (1941), in which the character played by Cary Grant confessed his real crimes at length, dissipating Joan Fontaine's suspicions that he had been trying to murder her. ("The idea of 'suspicion' is...the psychological equivalent of the 'exchange' whose moral dimension we will be studying,"[15] say the exegetes.) The sequence, which ended with Fontaine expressing skepticism about her husband's promised reformation by looking at the camera and raising her eyebrow, was rejected by preview audiences and replaced with a sped-up form of the same confession after a scary ride along a cliff overlooking the sea.

After Suspicion the main variations on the theme are Shadow of a Doubt (1943) ("The young girl doesn't believe herself to be guilty, does not act like a guilty person, but...by the discovery she makes of a fundamental flaw in the universe... the innocent, at the same time, loses her innocence"[16]), Notorious (1946) ("The unhappiness of the two protagonists comes from the fact that, victims of their mutual prejudices, they refuse to speak the 'word' that could save them"[17]), Spellbound (1945) ("Hitchcock is interested in the very principle of psychoanalysis—he sees in it the equivalent of the 'confession' that will supply the theme of Under Capricorn and I Confess"[18]), The Paradine Case (1947) ("Gregory Peck cannot cleanse his shame except by public confession"[19]), and Rope (1948), where a free-thinking teacher realizes that he shares in the guilt of two students who have put his ideas into practice by committing an unmotivated murder.

Despite all these interesting variations, write Rohmer and Chabrol, "the transference of guilt theme will find in Under Capricorn a more elo-

quent, purely cinematic expression,"[20] and this would happen after Hitchcock, in 1946, reengaged with Our Two Consciences, bought the property from Louis Verneuil, and began thinking about how to turn it into a film.

### From *Our Two Consciences* to *I Confess*

So far the substitution of Our Two Consciences for an immaterial archetype, arriving at some point "in the early '30s" like a deus ex machina, has not done much to complicate and refine the Platonic approach. But did the archetype really arrive in such a transcendent form?

Biographer Patrick McGilligan—reluctant like many Hitchcock scholars to accept the Rohmer-Chabrol reading of I Confess as a central work, and an overtly religious one—argues that Hitchcock was drawn to the play by the possibility of doing a thriller denouncing capital punishment.[21] If that were so, however, he would almost certainly have eventually made a film against capital punishment. He was stubborn about repeating an idea whose first incarnation had been spoiled (in this case, he felt, by studio-imposed compromises) until he got it right.

But there was foreign matter of another kind adhering to the divine pattern when Hitchcock first encountered it. While there can be no doubt that Father Pieux in the play is a Christ figure, his *imitatio Christi* is subsumed by a story that can only be described as political.

Paul Anthelme was a pen name used by journalist Paul Bourde, an editor of the review Le Temps, who is barely remembered today as a schoolmate of Arthur Rimbaud. A professional man of letters, Bourde kept up with Rimbaud after leaving Europe and abandoning poetry. There is a letter in which Bourde, who never really liked his classmate's work, informs him that he is becoming a cult favorite with immature young poets and offers him the equivalent of half a penny a word to write some new poems for Le Temps. Rimbaud suggested in his next letter that an advance of 4,500 francs would be more appropriate, and the correspondence broke off.

Bourde, a conservative Catholic, did not share Rimbaud's admiration for the 1871 Paris Commune, the May '68 of the 19th century—in fact he wrote, under the pen name Paul Delion, a whole book to discredit that anti-royalist uprising. His character sketches of the leaders of the rebellion all tend to illustrate the thesis that "men, some from conviction, others from ambition, go around spreading socialist and egalitarian ideas… *[but these ideas] have an effect exactly contrary to their stated aim*… So, these are ideas which must be destroyed, and the men who spread them must be combated. That is the task of the endangered class: the bourgeoisie."[22] This turns out to be the thesis of *Nos deux consciences*, where the *imitatio Christi* becomes part of a right-wing political argument.

*Nos deux consciences* is theater of ideas, a genre to which the young Hitchcock had been partial—he admired John Galsworthy and made an excellent film of Galsworthy's *The Skin Game* (1931), about the collision of aristocratic and bourgeois values in a land deal. It would have been clear to him that the "two consciences" of the title were sacred and secular and that the priest's conscience trumps the socialist politician's conscience, which produces "*an effect exactly contrary to [its] stated aim*," to paraphrase Bourde's thesis in the book about the Commune, whereas by following the will of the all-seeing Deity, Michel saves his own soul and the soul of a murderer. (In dramatizing his thesis, Bourde seems to have blended the Christian idea of sin with the Greek equivalent, *hamartia*, used by Aristotle in his theory of tragedy, which means literally "missed aim.")

This plot twist is preserved in the movie, where Father Logan's youthful (preordination) sweetheart Ruth Grandfort (Anne Baxter) decides over her politician husband's objections to confess that Logan was with her in order to give him an alibi, and her good action misfires in the same way. By revealing that Villette, the murdered man, was blackmailing her about her youthful fling with Michael Logan (the reason for their meeting the night of the murder), she only succeeds in giving the police a motive for Logan to have killed Villette. Hitchcock kept Bourde's ironic allegory but

switched meanings: in the film Bourde's "two consciences" become the opposition between profane love (Ruth) and sacred love (Michael).

The film Hitchcock wanted to make on this theme would have been quite consistent with the youthful mindset revealed in *The Skin Game* and the Sean O'Casey adaptation *Juno and the Paycock* (1930), which he made in the early 1930s, just before he encountered Bourde's play. These early sound films include "daring" reflections that are typical of the breast-beating young Catholic intellectuals are wont to indulge in—characters are driven by suffering to cry out that God does not exist, or that He is responsible for the evils that beset His creatures, and even for their sins, but these blasphemies are chastened and corrected by the dramatic context.

In *I Confess* Hitchcock had intended to posit an extreme case—the priest dies in the end—and weave out of it a theodicy, justifying the ways of God to Man. To up the moral ante, he had even thrown in the notion that the priest had sinned with Ruth Grandfort before his ordination, fathering an illegitimate child with her and driving his own brother to suicide.

Verneuil's first treatment stuck like glue to Bourde's plot, except for transposing the story to a small village outside San Francisco and making the killer a Mexican. But in his second treatment the priest himself becomes the father of the bastard—presumably at Hitchcock's behest, because this idea, like the priest's execution, was one he fought for against the studio and the censor, albeit with less hope of winning his point. (Concerning the priest's death, Hitchcock explained in a 1948 letter to a Catholic fan who had heard an early, garbled account of the project on the radio that the downbeat ending "may be changed if the murderer confesses and saves the priest." He then added: "But this premise would weaken our story.")

Also introduced in Verneuil's second draft: 1) a flashback in which there is still a brother, Philippe, and a triangle that ends with the girl in Michel's arms and Philippe a suicide, sending Michel into holy orders, after which he learns that he has a child; 2) a flashback scene where Michel gives extreme unction to his child, who is dying; and 3) a prologue and epilogue where we see a new chapel being dedicated to Michel's memory after his execution and exoneration. Verneuil explains, "In his omnipotence, the Lord, seemingly, wanted the culprit punished, but wanted also the martyrdom of the priest. In all Christian hearts, the memory of his death, so simple and so great, remains immaculate and shall live forever."

The priest's death and the killer's confession at the door of the prison stayed in the script for a long time, but Hitchcock waffled on the matter of the illegitimate child. In the 1947 draft he wrote with Alma Reville, his wife, it goes back to being the brother's child, and this solution is kept in the William Rose draft (August 11, 1948). Then the idea that it is the priest's child is resurrected in the version by Paul Vincent Carroll (May 5, 1950), with dialogue by playwright George Tabori, and the rewrite Hitchcock did after that with Barbara Keon (May 17, 1952).

The Hitchcock-Keon draft was the film he would have made if Jack Warner hadn't finally told him to discard two ideas he cherished or give up the project. The publicity flap when Hitchcock's first choice for the part of Ruth Grandfort arrived from Sweden with an illegitimate child in tow—a chilling recollection, for the studio, of Ingrid Bergman's troubles at the time of *Under Capricorn*— no doubt stiffened Warner's resolve not to make a film about a priest with an illegitimate child, even if the priest did die at the end. Both ideas had to go, and the fact that Hitchcock was willing to sacrifice them to get the project made suggests that, of all the ideas in the mix, the one that Rohmer and Chabrol made synonymous with his name was, in the last analysis, his reason for making *I Confess*.

Although Bourde's right-wing ideas seem to have interested him not at all, the theme of sacred and secular that was now embodied in the contrast between Michael and silly, romantic Ruth did have political resonances in Quebec, where Hitchcock had chosen to set the story. Ruth Grandfort's husband is still a liberal—he is arguing in favor of equal pay for female teachers when we first see him through Ruth's adoring eyes—and the opposi-

tion between Ruth's well-intentioned confession and Father Logan's refusal to speak could be read as an allegory of contemporary social conflicts in the Quebec of Premier Maurice Duplessis. Murray Pomerance observes:

The social and moral tensions imported to Quebecois society by the ascendancy of Duplessis to power in 1944, and highlighted by his longstanding dispute with clerical dominion…continued into the contemporary age a philosophical and economic struggle that had its roots in feudal Europe ….Was it holy ordinance or secular statute that would establish and frame relations between the sexes, between good men and bad, between crime and normality?[23]

Perhaps this explains why the Archbishop of Ottawa, when Sidney Bernstein showed him a version of the script that contained both the bastard and the execution of the priest, smiled and said, "Ca, c'est du cinéma!"[24]

But the film the archbishop okayed is not the film Hitchcock finally made, and for that the French can thank Jack Warner, because the shift of emphasis from theodicy to redemption through confession contributed to the unfolding of the structure that was taking shape while Hitchcock struggled to get the script of *I Confess* right.

In fact, if we go back and lay side by side the chronology of the development of *I Confess* and that of the other films being made during this period, we can see that the evolving story of *I Confess* was already part of the DNA of two other key transference-of-guilt films, *Under Capricorn* and *Strangers on a Train*.

During the making of *Under Capricorn* and *Stage Fright* (1950), according to McGilligan, Leslie Storm was hired to work on *I Confess* and fired, and Graham Greene was approached to do a draft and said no, but no real progress was made beyond the 1947 and 1948 drafts Hitchcock had done with Alma and William Rose, which overlapped with the actual writing of *Under Capricorn*.[25]

In Helen Simpson's novel *Under Capricorn*, Hattie Flusky's confession that she, and not her husband, killed her brother comes one-third of the way through the book and is given no dramatic weight at all.[26] The fact that Hitchcock already had in hand a property where the climax of the story is a murderer's public confession after an innocent man has been executed, all within the framework of the Roman Catholic sacrament of confession, must have had some influence on his adaptation of *Under Capricorn*, even if it was released five years before *I Confess*.

Then in 1950, while Hitchcock was working on *Strangers on a Train*, he commissioned a new script for *I Confess* by George Tabori that was being finished even as the director was leaving for New York and Washington to film location scenes for *Strangers*, armed with a temporary script for that film that he had whipped up with Barbara Keon, a former Selznick employee. Keon subsequently helped knock *I Confess* into shape after Tabori and William Archibald, who ended up with screen credit, had done their drafts.

*Strangers* marks the next phase after *Under Capricorn* of the revelation of the transference theme, which is geometrically embodied in Patricia Highsmith's novel. But *I Confess* had already been in development for two years when Hitchcock read Highsmith's book and bought it to kick off his deal as producer-director at Warner Bros., and the two films were closely intertwined in their evolution after that.

In particular, both presented the same problem: how to effect the real murderer's confession, which would restore the innocence of the *faux coupable*, given that Bruno Anthony was insane and Father Logan, at this point in the development of *I Confess*, was still slated to die for the crime the sacristan Keller had admitted to under the seal of the confessional.

By October of 1950—in the Hitchcock-Keon temporary script for *Strangers* and Carroll's draft of *I Confess*—the solution was to make the murderer's confession an *acte manqué*, like Mr. Memory's confession in *The 39 Steps*. Bruno accidentally confessing while babbling to the police after the merry-go-round crash, and Keller still hysterically confessing as the murderer does in Bourde's play when the notice that Father Logan has been executed is posted on the prison gates.

Better versions of this solution would be found in the script of *Strangers* that Hitchcock hammered out with Ben Hecht protégée Czenzi Ormonde during filming and in the script of *I Confess* that was finally produced by ping-ponging drafts back and forth between Hitchcock, Keon, Archibald, and Tabori before and during filming in Quebec: the lighter falling from Bruno's hand as he dies, and Keller blurting out the truth after mistakenly concluding that Logan has denounced him to the police.

If anything, that pattern emerged more clearly once it was decided that Keller's involuntary confession would clear Logan just before Keller is killed by the police, setting the stage for what appears in retrospect to have been the only possible ending for the film: Keller's dying confession and Logan's intoned absolution. Simple, unexpected, and breathtakingly right.

NOTE: This article is based on script materials and other archives of the production of *I Confess* at the Warner Bros. Archives, University of Southern California. A rudimentary early version appeared in *Senses of Cinema*. All translations from the French are mine. My particular theory of creation through reading is developed at greater length in the article "Tredici modi di guardare uno zombi," *George A. Romero*, ed. Giulia D'Agnolo Vallan (Torino: Associazione Cinema Giovani, 2001), 109–125. The critic who has done the most to advance this way of understanding Hitchcock is Ken Mogg, whose discussions of literary and cinematic sources for the work can be found in his book *The Alfred Hitchcock Story* (London: Titan Books, 1999) and on his Web site at www.labyrinth. net.au/~muffin. The reader may also find it useful to consult Erich Auerbach, "'Figura,'" in *Scenes from the Drama of European Literature* (New York: Meridian Books, 1959), 11–76, the indispensable scholarly reference for discussions of figural meaning, and Northrop Frye, *Anatomy of Criticism*, (New York: Atheneum, 1968), 41–43, on dramatic forms in which a *pharmakos* or scapegoat is the protagonist.

Alfred Hitchcock and his wife and regular collaborator, Alma Reville, preparing to eat some cake. Still courtesy of the Academy of Motion Picture Arts and Sciences. Rights courtesy of Universal Studios Licensing LLLP.

# 5

# Hitchcock à la Carte: Menus, Marketing, and the Macabre

JAN OLSSON

Q: If you were going to be murdered, how would you choose to have it done?
A: Well, there are many nice ways: Eating is a good one.[1]

In the late 1920s in Britain, Alfred Hitchcock emerged as a cinematic wunderkind, and his showmanship soon turned film marketing into an artful form of self-promotion. In press conferences Hitchcock slyly delivered mischievous talking points and head-on provocations, which generated buzz and an endless loop of qualifications and clarifications. From the mid-1930s, Hitchcock's public persona was as formidable as his films, and Hollywood slowly emerged on his radar, not least after his summer outing to New York City in 1937. The Hitchcock family came to the city for a veritable Roman holiday: a systematic and very public mapping of the city's best tables. Hitchcock already enjoyed a strong reputation in the United States as a director of first-rate thrillers, but his accomplishments on the screen were overshadowed by his gastronomic adventures, which set the tone for a key aspect of the future Hitchcock reception. Decades later, television emerged as a prime arena for turning Hitchcock into a cultural icon. Here he found an ideal outlet for his onscreen persona cleverly devised by James Allardice for the bookend segments.

The plastic Hitchcock figure functioned as an askew spokesperson for a malleable oeuvre effortlessly crossing boundaries between forms of expression and in the process gradually undermining cultural hierarchies and high-low distinctions. This malleability is evident in the endless amount of theories mobilized to academically account for the Hitchcock domain, which has turned into a benchmark for the scholarly industry in its fine arts, philosophical, and media precincts. Parallel to his marketing of himself as master of ceremonies in a wide sense, for example as artist in control of all aspects of a production, Hitchcock emerged as the prototypical auteur in the critical discourse. Alfred Hitchcock covered the cultural spectrum: cameo figure, television host, brand name for mystery novels, auteur, marketer on and off screen, and iconic rotund silhouette. His ubiquity helped propel his films—and the frames and sequences from the films, the images and sketches created by Hitchcock and his collaborators, the photographs of Hitchcock himself—into galleries and museums. For a Hollywood director, Hitchcock appropriated a vast realm beyond Hollywood, and his work changed both art institutions and the role and importance of popular culture. Alongside artist Andy Warhol, Sir Alfred is the rare person who has straddled both these spheres. Like

Warhol, Hitchcock understood the importance of being immediately identifiable. For Hitchcock this meant a lifelong association with his embonpoint and the food that made it.

After his visit to New York City, Hitchcock's body loomed large as an unwieldy emblem for—and the order is telling—his appetite and mastery in dishing up thrilling suspense. A decade later, after leaving the David O. Selznick studio, Hitchcock was on the verge of turning into a small franchise of his own via his Transatlantic Pictures and Warner Bros. Further down the road, when Hitchcock began hosting his television shows in the mid-1950s, he was a media empire in the making. His readily recognizable bodily profile—melodiously marching from charcoal sketch via shadow to on-screen presence in formal attire—became a veritable trademark for his macabre televisual panache.[2] The clout and bargaining power garnered by Hitchcock through the television series' global success awarded him Universal Studios' third heaviest stock portfolio when he traded his television company, Shamley, together with the rights to *Psycho* (1960), for shares in the Music Corporation of America (MCA)-led film studio in 1962.[3]

The eccentric Hitchcock figure on the small screen in combination with his offbeat off-screen ventures kept him in the limelight on a weekly basis throughout a decade. Food and eating ventures had played a prominent part in the marketing of the persona from the gastronomic holiday of 1937 up until Hitchcock was presented as television host in 1955, so why not address these matters as they relate to his role as a television host?

The irreverent topic for this text is the intersection of the televisual and culinary realms in marketing and reception discourses and Hitchcock's mastery in selling the food-conscious Hitchcock figure in all imaginable contexts. This essay will address the discursive realm and promotional dialectics concerning culinary and bodily matters gravitating around Hitchcock. We will chart the acerbic body talk framing him in the United States and his negotiating of this discourse as part of a shrewdly self-styled public persona, which turned out to have a universal appeal. We will also discuss how the culinary purview is intertwined with his upbeat approach to murder, inherently English according to Hitchcock and oftentimes subsumed under the plastic generic adjective "macabre." In both the national and global marketing of a Hitchcock persona, the television series' impact cannot be overestimated.

*

Television played a decisive role by offering the host a unique weekly platform to address the nation—and soon many other countries too—on all matters Hitchcock. These carefully scripted segments molded the Hitchcockian persona by bestowing upon the public conception of him a set of signifiers he had to abide by for the rest of his life. The split between an invisible real Hitchcock and the contours of the public conception was jestingly addressed as a thin-stout dichotomy in an after-dinner speech scripted by his television writer, which we will return to below. The bulk of the promotional endeavors during his Hollywood career were built around the constructed Hitchcock persona and its translation to the body of work, which gradually was pivoted differently after the success of his television series. The Sunday night performances in American living rooms turned Hitchcock into a popular figure. Henceforth he was an inescapable media fixture—on primetime television, in marketing for his films, on the covers of his mystery magazine and his books.

Hitchcock always positioned himself at least on par with the stars of his films—cattle or not. After being happily reframed for the small screen, he was more than ever the superstar around whom the individual films gravitated and a bona fide master of media ceremonies to boot. To his longstanding cameo habit were added elaborate publicity spins: for *Vertigo* (1958) these included a press junket in San Francisco featuring a post-screening dinner at Ernie's followed the next day by Hitchcock serving as a tour guide to the film's landmark locations; for *Psycho*, in addition to radio spots and advertisements, Hitchcock was employed as a cardboard figure advising moviegoers to arrive early because no one would be admitted

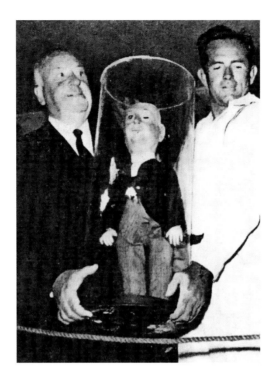

Alfred Hitchcock and his replica in a time capsule to be buried on a Florida beach.

Although Hitchcock is now widely regarded as the often somber master of suspense, scribes persisted, throughout his career, in routinely and comically foregrounding his body as they had since 1937. Newspaper journalists and magazine writers seemingly tried to outwit each other in their merciless stabs at Hitchcock's bulky frame and bodily peculiarities—and Hitchcock, willingly or not, elected to play along, or even outplay them, by adding self-disparaging remarks to his repertory of talking points. As we will see later in this essay, such tactics hark back to his last years in England, when he reportedly at times entertained the press wearing a dressing gown and silk pajamas that "accentuated his girth."[6] Such sartorial informality was never displayed in the United States, but when back in London for *Frenzy* (1972) in the 1970s, Hitchcock entertained journalists one-on-one dressed in a blue bathrobe with "matching slippers."[7]

Hitchcock was a winning proposition after his television success from 1955 and onwards, but his next two films, *The Wrong Man* (1956) and *Vertigo*, were far from smash hits at the box office. Critically, he still had his predictable detractors among highbrow reviewers, especially in the *New Yorker*.[8] The shift from big-budget spectacle after *North by Northwest* (1959) to the gritty, black-and-white television look for the low-budget, high-grossing *Psycho* was a one-time effort, albeit one with immense ramifications for the horror genre as well as the overall genre balance in Hollywood— and not least for Hitchcock's coffers and position within the industry. Hitchcock himself, however, reverted back to big budgets and new, challenging production constraints for his next exercise in horror, while his television franchise continued to print money on a weekly basis, but without Hitchcock taking on directorial stints after "I Saw the Whole Thing," which aired on October 11, 1962. The television format had recently changed from the half hour of *Alfred Hitchcock Presents* to the *Alfred Hitchcock Hour*, which opened in the fall of 1962, when the show bounced back to CBS after two seasons at NBC.

late. Hitchcock also added a new performance format to his cinematic repertory, the trailers, emulating his host segments on the television show.

Hitchcock had always enjoyed promotional globetrotting for his films. In the wake of the worldwide television success, he was a big ticket on all continents and on top of his game. Moreover, he was game and unfazed enough to take on virtually any type of puffery. When his television sponsor, for example, came up with the harebrained idea to bury a replica of Hitchcock in a time capsule on a beach in Florida, the television host cheerfully participated.[4] Previously, he had hosted a much-publicized ghost-haunted house party in New York—more about that later—and a luncheon party in Beverly Hills, where the guests invited to the Brown Derby were surprised to find themselves transported to a local jail for the meal.[5] Such brouhaha promulgated the overall public conception of Hitchcock the prankster and reinforced an overarching frame for his television series. The host segments for his shows set the stage for the eccentric and macabre stunts he occasionally hosted off-screen for the benefit of the press as lead-ins to the show.

*Alfred Hitchcock Presents* opened on CBS in October 1955, a couple of weeks ahead of the premiere of *The Trouble with Harry* (1955), this "curiously whimsical thing," as Bosley Crowther put it.[9] At the time, Hitchcock was planning his final vehicle for Warner Bros., *The Wrong Man*, after having moved over to Paramount for a long-term deal. The mid-1950s was a very productive time for Hitchcock: *Rear Window* was released August 1, 1954; *To Catch a Thief* appeared in late July 1955; and *The Man Who Knew Too Much* was scheduled for release in May 1956. All were based on screenplays by John Michael Hayes (as was *The Trouble with Harry*).

Whimsical or not, *The Trouble with Harry*, a perennial Hitchcock favorite, was, in fact, screened for the writer hired for scripting the introductions and epilogues for the television show as exemplary in terms of the tone sought for the director's appearance on the small screen. Whimsical is only one of numerous epithets that come to mind apropos Hitchcock's television persona as constructed by James Allardice, who scripted a decade's worth of Hitchcock interventions. Allardice had won an Emmy in March 1955 for his contribution as comedy cowriter of *The George Gobel Show* at NBC, which gives a hint of the sort of material Hitchcock and his people were gunning for. The encounter between Allardice's tongue-in-cheek scripts and Hitchcock's peerless delivery proved to be a perfect fit. Even outside the shows, Allardice contributed to many of Hitchcock's public performances and scripted trailers featuring Hitchcock, including those for *North by Northwest*, *Psycho*, and *The Birds* (1963), up until the writer's death shortly after the end of the television run.

Throughout the years, Hitchcock dealt with interviews by recounting and embellishing a fairly limited repertory of anecdotes, stories, yarns, and biographical notes bearing on his professional practices and personal life: his mother frightening him as an infant, his father sending him to jail for five minutes, what glacial women could do when alone with a man in the backseat of a cab, the differences between suspense and mystery (often outlined with the example of a bomb ticking unbe-

knownst to the characters but with the audience aware of it), what a McGuffin is not, whether actors are cattle or not, that the shooting of a film is boring and routine while the fun and ingenuity are in the preparation. It is within this repertory of stories that the recurrent references to his body, tastes, and diets reside, and it was by tapping this pool that Allardice constructed the popular persona of Alfred Hitchcock on television in roughly 370 variations over a decade.

Those few weekly minutes featuring Hitchcock as television host not only bookended the short dramas but proved to be an indispensable part of the package, besides being the points of suture for the diverse anthology format. As John Crosby poignantly mused, "The best thing about *Alfred Hitchcock Presents* is Alfred Hitchcock presenting."[10] Crosby's tagline for the piece, "Macabre Merriment," is right on target, for both the television show and all the other brands of entertainment Hitchcock indulged in. Overall, the television hosting was a crucial part of the process of reinventing Hitchcock's image. By obliquely appropriating and toying with the ubiquitous body discourse, the host segments shifted emphasis to a macabre convergence between eating *à la française* and killing *à l'anglaise*.[11] "Menu" thus became a master trope with Hitchcock as chef in charge of serving up lethal gourmet suspense even when his *sous-chefs* directed.

To further bolster his penchant for the macabre, Hitchcock hosted a ghost-haunted house party in New York prior to the shooting of *The Wrong Man*. The advertising agency Young & Rubicam, working for his television sponsor, Bristol-Myers, had scouted a properly spooky location for the party. Hitchcock eventually settled for a house, 7 East 80th Street, and a date, March 7, 1956.[12] Those invited received a preview of the offerings on the backside of the tombstone-shaped invitation card. The out-of-the-ordinary menu promised "morbid morgue mussels, suicide suzettes, consommé de cobra, vicious-soise, home-fried homicide, ragout of reptile, charcoal broiled same-witch-legs, corpse croquettes, barbequed banshee, opium omelette, stuffed stiff with hard sauce, gibbeted giblets, mobster thermidor, tormented tortillas, ghoulish goulash, blind bats en casserole, python pudding, fresh-cut lady fingers, Bloody Marys, Dead Grand-dad, formaldehyde frappé."[13] A ghoul placed in a hearse maintained atmospheric vigil outside the premises, while inside a Charles Addams butler offered the guests the comforting welcome greeting "Drop Dead." Scores of caskets, eerie illumination, stuffed birds, dusty cobwebs, knifed portraits leaking blood, glowing footprints on the walls, recorded voices, funeral music played on theremin, and flower arrangements added to the creepy ambience.[14] The food offerings and the menu's overall association with death, dismemberment, and cannibalism apparently failed to amuse the guests, Donald Spoto reports.[15] Not least since Hitchcock on television and in the press came across as a diehard gourmet.

Menu-wise, a couple of his television shows upped the ante by featuring bodies as foodstuff in the manner of his party offerings. In "The Specialty of the House" (aired December 13, 1959), the coveted dish at a gourmet club turns out to require human flesh, which in this case is the story's obligatory twist ending.[16] Thus, Lamb Armistran was only served when a member of the club was killed off. In "Arthur," an episode directed by Hitchcock (aired September 27, 1959), the processed dead body of Arthur's former girlfriend is used for chicken food. When later ending up on the plates, the chickens apparently taste marvelous. Hitchcock several times discussed Lord Dunsany's famous "Two Bottles of Relish" as a short story the studios and networks would not allow him to do. This is a story that does not spell out cannibalism, but only such a reading can crack its doubled-edged enigma. One of Hitchcock's host segments operates in a similar register. When he opens his meat freezer with meat cleaver in hand, human bodies are hanging inside the cold storage ("Triumph," aired December 14, 1964).

Hitchcock appears as a chef in the introduction to "Conversation over a Corpse" (aired November 18, 1956), an episode that's reminiscent of the serialized glitch in *The Trouble with Harry*. Here, however, two elderly sisters do not have to dispose

of a corpse, but, rather, in a series of attempts try to turn their scheming real-estate agent into a corpse. One of them eventually manages to cleverly get rid of both him and her sister before Hitchcock returns to cooking in the epilogue. "The Cadaver" (aired November 29, 1963) offers a storyline again somewhat akin to *The Trouble with Harry*. Here the disposal of a dead body that shows up in the wrong place is dealt with in a more radical fashion than the annoying Harry was—and without any form of whimsical merriment. Finally, in "The Last Request" (November 24, 1957), Hitchcock himself, sitting in a big kettle, is prepared as a dish in the prologue; in the epilogue he sulks after having been dropped from the menu and substituted with a woman.

In numerous contexts Hitchcock repeated his stance that murder, in the English tradition, could be fun, while "murders in U.S. lack charm."[17] Perhaps Hitchcock's sprightly attitude toward murder is most evident when he depicted it in culinary terms. *Psycho*, for example, which features a cozy little meal prepared by Norman for Marion before Mother shows up for the subsequent shower scene, was marketed in menu-like terms in a photojournalistic spin allegedly authored by Hitchcock:

May I recommend a meal fit for a killer? Start with the antipasto of one passionate peccadillo and 40,000 greenbacks. The main dish: mayhem, rare. Now you know the menu of my new film-flam—*Psycho*. But as you'll see it, much depends on the chef."

A series of photos by Eugene Cook with captions provide further plot points:

"Take two lovers…mix well with one odd fellow…blend in one rainy night…and a knife [Hitchcock threatened by gigantic knife; in the next image outside the house, his head seems to float in the darkness]…season with a ghost house and a corpse…one quivering culprit…and a witless witness…add one scheming director [Hitchcock with hat in what looks like dark a circus ring, stark light, his outfit picked up from the cameo appearance]…and the plot boils.[18]

The tongue-in-cheek outline, which expands on the captions, is still succinct in the manner of the

## blend in one rainy night... and a knife

Tony's small motel is hardly the kind that inspires soggy songs about wishing wells. But 'tis a retreat where a distraught chap can gnaw his nails when knives flash in the dark. Y'know, there's nothing like a blade to make you look sharp. Here now, boy! Watch that bread knife!

From the marketing campaign for *Psycho* (1960), Alfred Hitchcock's recipe for suspense (printed in *Coronet* [September 1960].) Courtesy of Universal Studios Licensing LLLP.

## season with a ghost house and a corpse...

Don't you admire my taste in homes? Think what Charles Addams and I could do in the suburbs! Crypt-level haunted houses! This one is a fine example of 20th-century Grotesque. But the architecture of an undressed young corpse gave Tony Perkins a few embarrassing moments. "She keeps winking at me," he complained.

## one quivering culprit...

## and a witless witness...

But which is which? That is the question. Why is Tony running? You'd run, too, if cadavers checked into your motel. A fellow could lose his A.A.A. endorsement. And why is Janet upset? Is she one of the cadavers?

television segments. The multiplicity of roles for Hitchcock is a key element in the photo essay: as chef/director hunkering down under the knife and in his cameo costume against a backdrop not seen in the film. The carefree mixing of thrilling ingredients draws on the macabre intersection between food preparation and palatable thriller fare dished up with good cheer calculated to offset the unsavory aspects of the story.

In 1956, at the time of the haunted house party, Hitchcock had not yet galvanized the accoutrements of the television show into an inescapable public image for the host; otherwise Charles Gounod's "Funeral March of a Marionette" would have been mandatory background music for the macabre dinner event. Decades later when Hitchcock shot what turned out to be his last film, *Family Plot* (1976), reporters were treated to a luncheon at a cemetery built on the Universal Studios backlot. "Scattered about the lawn" the guests found tombstones labeled with their names, and "waitresses veiled in black [were] dispensing Bloody Marys; and an organist [was] pumping away at Gounod's 'Funeral March of a Marionette.'"

True to form, Hitchcock posed for photographers "beside his own gravestone, which, typically, was decorated with a bust that wore his own pendulous visage." Gregg Kilday's account in the *Los Angeles Times* posed the key question "What becomes a legend most?" Discerningly, he concluded the answer was "a simple and unwavering allegiance to the Hitchcock public image," which was defined by the trappings of his television hosting and the intertwining of the macabre and the humorous, a winning, inherently English, combination.[19] Juicy murders and serial killers carried an aura of ghastly glamour in Britain, Hitchcock claimed, outlined in all their fascinating hideousness in the courts and the press. Hitchcock ventured a series of sociological observations in an article in the *New York Times* concerning the Brits' taste for murder. Overcrowded living conditions allegedly generate a high level of regard for privacy; thus the wife can be conveniently killed off and disposed of without prying neighbors nosing around or watching through rear windows. Sum-

ming up decades later, Hitchcock estimated that "during my television series, we buried at least 200 women in the cellar over a 10-year period."[20] In a differently balanced account, women had allegedly committed 99 crimes during the 134 weeks the show at that time had been on the air.[21]

The television show continued to mold Hitchcock's public persona even after it ended, due to the eternal return of episodes in syndicated reruns. And Hitchcock continued to play the part of Hitchcock with relish. In the 1970s Richard Schickel observed that Hitchcock did not promote his films but himself, "or, more properly, the public persona constructed as carefully as any of his movie plots. That persona—the slightly macabre, perversely jolly fat man—emerged as the host of his extremely popular television shows in the 1950s."[22] The Hitchcockian food obsession and the American press's interest in his body in turn informed his host segments on television. His obesity and his ravenous eating had provided coordinates and points of departure for the American Hitchcock discourse since 1937. The prime topic for the host segments was the overall marketing of a conception of the host, the negotiation of the public persona of Alfred Hitchcock.

*

His cameo mania, a signature device for Hitchcock movies starting with *The Lodger* (1927), has always constituted an interesting type of game for new generations of fans; these days many Web sites give the game away.[23] Eventually Hitchcock wanted to divert the audience's attention from his cameo appearance by having it over with in the opening of the films. He consistently adhered to the format established in his silent films and over the decades never awarded himself a word as cameo figure. In the previously mentioned after-dinner speech from 1965, scripted by Allardice, Hitchcock waxed eloquently on the question "Who Is the Real Alfred Hitchcock?" His answer throws us back to the cameos and the inveterate Hitchcock issue of obesity. According to Hitchcock:

There seems to be a widespread impression that I am stout. I can see you share my amusement at

A restful moment. Courtesy of the Swedish Film Institute, Stockholm.

this obvious distortion of the truth.... I am certain that you are wondering how such a story got started. It began nearly 40 years ago. As you know, I make a brief appearance in each of my pictures. One of the earliest of these was *The Lodger,* the story of Jack the Ripper. My appearance called for me to walk up the stairs of the rooming house. Since my walk-ons in subsequent films would be equally strenuous—boarding buses, playing chess, etc.—I asked for a stunt man. Casting, in an unusual lack of perception, hired this fat man! The rest is history. HE became the public image of Alfred Hitchcock. Changing the image was impossible. Therefore I had to conform to the image. [...] As you know, I still remain a prisoner of the old image. They say that inside every fat man is a thin man trying desperately to get out. Now you know that the thin man is the real Alfred Hitchcock.[24]

This negotiation of Hitchcock's identity and, more generally, the role his body played as butt of an endless string of cruel jokes—and self-mockery—from the very moment he arrived in the United States are discursive points of reference impossible to ignore in the contexts of promotion and reception. In a 1939 article Paul Speegle implied that the reason Hitchcock's body is of such interest is that it is incongruous: "One would picture Alfred Hitchcock the eminent English director as a tall, hawk-faced man, slim of build, whose long fingers, when they are not toying with the stem of a cocktail glass, are gliding deftly over the still-warm body of a corpse, searching for clues." In contrast to "the image we conjured up…Mr. Hitchcock is actually a round, roly-poly man, possessed of several chins which lie in chuckling folds upon a nonexistent neck."[25]

In the American context, Hitchcock's physique turned into an inescapable topic after the gluttony reported on during his 1937 visit; henceforth he had to run the discursive gauntlet of incisive body jokes. When he arrived in the United States, he told an interviewer after returning to England, reporters "took one look at my shape when I came down the gangplank and started interviewing me on food. I told them my favorite dish was steak *à la mode*."[26] The story did not end there, however, and the most famous and trendsetting of the articles from Hitchcock's visit was penned with gusto from inside the renowned Club 21, whose famous chefs later prepared cinematic takeout food for the gourmet dinner Grace Kelly's character ordered in *Rear Window* (1954). When dining at 21, the witty journalist H. Allen Smith joined the Hitchcocks.

**Hitchcock in his element in New York City in 1937 together with (from left) his wife, Alma Reville; his assistant Joan Harrison; and his daughter, Patricia.**

Hitchcock is served a macabre
dish in Stockholm in 1960.
Courtesy of the Swedish Film
Institute, Stockholm.

piercing eyes that peek elfishly out of a rubicund face. When he smiles, his chins all smile with him, one after another.[29]

After a thorough investigation of multiple eateries—Club 21, Waldorf-Astoria, St. Regis, and Gallagher's among others—his "worst fears were set at rest," he told reporters when back the following year. "American steaks were worth crossing the Atlantic for," Hitchcock mused, and he even declared himself willing to "barter England's steak-and-kidney pie for a double order of Yankee ice cream."[30] The ice cream at the Waldorf was apparently heavenly and the T-bone steak at Gallagher's a "masterpiece," while American tea, however, was a total letdown.[31] Wine, in contrast, proved a pleasant surprise for someone fearing America could serve only something fit "for a fountain pen."[32] The bevy of reports from his ten gastronomic days in the United States in 1937 laid the foundation for virtually all articles in the popular press on Hitchcock, and according to a trade columnist, "in view of all the publicity Alfred Hitchcock has been receiving on his food preferences in the town's cabareateries," the name of Hitchcock's company should "be changed to GOURMAND-BRITISH."[33]

Dieting emerged as a topic when Hitchcock returned the following year and from New York embarked on his first visit to Hollywood. When dining with the *New York Sun*'s Eileen Creelman at Club 21, Hitchcock drew pictures of food for the benefit of the waiters while pensively telling the reporter that his "happy days of gourmandizing are over" due to doctor's orders. Hence champagne instead of hard liquor, still gigantic steaks, of course, but nothing else.[34] A lengthy write-up in the *New York Times* from this second visit elaborated on his masterful command of the screen melodrama and in a standard rhetorical thrust moved from pronouncing him the greatest director in this respect to the greatness of his body:

Mr. Hitchcock is a fat man (official displacement, 270 pounds), but only as King Edward VII was fat—that is to say, majestically. He has the appearance of being light on his feet, and picking away among the complicated technical pitfalls of one

Smith's account of the regale devoured by Hitchcock is a classic, a veritable ur-scene for the director's gourmet-cum-gourmand approach to eating. Before rounding out his meal with tea and brandy, Hitchcock had ordered three servings of steak, each followed by ice cream. According to Smith, Hitchcock started his day with ice cream flavored with a dash of brandy for breakfast and invariably had a sizable steak for lunch.[27] In an interview with Janet White a couple of days later, Hitchcock said he "refuses to diet or take any exercise. It makes me disgruntled." Per her interview his favorite "menu consists of meat, potatoes, and fruit." And he added more pensively, "I first started to put on weight when I took to drink. That doesn't mean what you think it does, for I take alcohol in moderation only. I've always been very particular about food. My mother told me that when I was very young she took me out of school because I objected to the cuisine."[28] The *New York Times* offered its spin on the director's girth on a similar note:

Mr. Hitchcock is a walking monument to the principle of uninhibited addiction to sack and capon, prime beef and flowing ale, and double helpings of ice cream. His free-floating, unconfined waistline is a triumph in embonpoint, and he scrutinizes the world, catching its moods and manners and filing them away for future availability, through bright, of his own top-grade mysteries he conveys the same gratifying impression: that of a very large and very solid personality walking among fragile things with the lightness and delicate precision of a cat.[35]

So established was the food discourse that when Hitchcock passed through New York *en route* in 1939 to start his work for Selznick, he was first and foremost identified as the "rotund gourmet" and only secondly as "outstanding director," preceded with a qualifying "also."[36] In 1943 Hitchcock, then in one of his less majestic stages, tried to counteract the discourse and exert damage control—or perhaps slyly further promulgate the buzz—as a guest columnist in the *New York Post*:

Ever since I began directing pictures, people have been told about a Hitchcock who eats steaks with alternate mouthfuls of ice cream three times a day…. To begin with, take that business about the steaks. I haven't the slightest notion where it started or who started it, but it has gained currency as Washington's cherry tree, by sheer force of repetition and for lack of denial. I suppose because I have bulk on my side, somebody came to the all-too-obvious conclusion that I must simply stuff myself with beefsteaks.[37]

Even a decade later, the pervasiveness of the food rumors prompted his studio to address the matter with explicit reference to the first round of texts. A Paramount Studio biography on Hitchcock dated April 1955 that was circulated to the press for several years addressed the subject by directly alluding to Smith's famous account from Club 21:

Out of a New York interview rose the typical fable that Hitchcock only eats beefsteak and ice cream in this country because he lacks confidence in the ability of the American chefs to create other viands. This, he now admits, was a culinary canard. While Hitch is not the enormous figure he used to be, he retains the double chin and round face which, with his bright blue eyes and bristly black hair, give him the appearance of an alert and intelligent cherub.[38]

Normally reticent about his private life, Hitchcock himself elected to recurrently refer to and joke about his body and weight, which spilled over to Allardice's scripting of his host segments.

Allardice's mordant wit took the sting out of the body discourse by claiming the genre for Hitchcock on his own terms, and the avalanche of press material is saturated with corporeal observations and body yarns spun by Hitchcock himself. For example, in a piece from 1962 wittily titled "Alfred Hitchcock Resents," he gets a chance to deliver niceties on all kinds of topics, including himself: "A few years ago, in Santa Rosa, California, I caught a side view of myself in a store window and screamed with fright. Since then I limit myself to a three-course dinner of appetizer, fish, and meat with only one bottle of vintage wine with each course."[39] During the shooting of *Shadow of a Doubt* (1943) in Santa Rosa, Hitchcock's obesity level peaked, hence the frightening reflection. Hitchcock rehashed the story and mixed in additional motifs when later interviewed by Oriana Fallaci. Says Hitchcock to Fallaci, who, impressed with his after-dinner habits of washing the dishes, had offered to marry him should he divorce:

The first thing I expect of my wife is to be good at cooking. Are you a good cook? My wife is an excellent cook, and I could die eating. The things that make me happiest in the world are eating, drinking, and sleeping. I sleep like a newborn babe. I drink like a fish, have you seen what a red face I have? And I eat like a pig. Even if it does make me look more and more like a porker myself. Some days ago, walking along in New York, I saw myself reflected in a window, and before I recognized myself, I let out a yell of fright. Then I called to my wife, "Who's that porker on two legs?" I didn't want to believe it when she replied, "It is you, dear."[40]

Thus Hitchcock and Allardice's writings further emphasized his self-designed signature drawing, which captured his rotund bodily profile in a few economic ink lines.[41] In the mid-1950s, Hitchcock had again shaken off a considerable amount of pounds accumulated since his last major weight-loss effort and was down to his all-time American low, 190 pounds. When promoting *Dial M for Murder* (1954) in London in April 1954, the press, according to Donald Spoto, was more interested in the director's physique than the film. Hitchcock claimed it had been "murder getting down to this weight, sheer masochism. For months it's been one meal a day—a lamb chop and few beans. And not a drop to drink."[42]

A prototypical joke devised by Allardice for a ghostwritten preface to a collection of stories perfectly captures the mode of flagellant witticisms Hitchcock delivered as host. In the preface Hitchcock tells us, "I was Johnny-come-lately to television, and some persons have claimed that I was waiting for the screens to become wide enough to accommodate me (an allegation which I stoutly deny)."[43] When his television show expanded from the half hour format of *Alfred Hitchcock Presents* to *The Alfred Hitchcock Hour* in the fall of 1962, Hitchcock commented on the change as a guest columnist in the *Morning Telegraph* in the same jocular tone: "It is not literally true that television viewers, during the coming season, will see twice as much Alfred Hitchcock as before. My diet forbids such a ghastly eventuality. At the same time that I am determined to remain a sylph of my former self, it is decidedly true that *The Alfred Hitchcock Hour,* as the title rather plainly implies, will endure for 60 minutes."[44]

Hitchcock's obesity was constantly joked about in Hollywood, especially up until his first dramatic weight loss after the making of *Shadow of a Doubt*. In *Sullivan's Travels*, Preston Sturges's 1941 comedy, there is a pregnant moment when Sullivan is finally recognized for who he is, a Hollywood director. He is immediately confronted with a set of questions concerning other directors. A young girl asks: Is Capra nice? Do you think Orson Welles is crazy? And is Hitchcock as fat as they say he is? Concerning the latter question, Sullivan quips, "Fatter." His producer Walter Wanger penned a very appreciative portrait of Hitchcock headlined "Hollywood Genius" but still of course sporting the established body facts: "Hitch is fat, forty, and full of fire," and looks like a "combination of a Sherlock Holmes and a Balzac overeating at the Ritz,"and "what he can do to a double-thick steak is no Hollywood secret."[45]

Indeed it is hard to imagine Hollywood not noticing Hitchcock's eating habits. After moving over to Hollywood, Hitchcock discovered Dave Chasen's restaurant in Beverly Hills, and for home eating he had acquired storage space at the Los Angeles Smoking and Curing Company for the shipments of English bacon and Dover sole he had arranged from the old country; these propelled him to the staggering figure of 365 pounds in 1939.[46] Having taken on additional weight, Hitchcock began to regularly wear a dark suit for "cosmetic camouflage."[47] From 1937 on, scale figures were a staple of the popular writing on Hitchcock, but the amount of pounds reported to readers was often widely conflicting. The figures and weight fluctuation are not important per se, but interesting as attempts at empirical anchoring and as a corporeal pretext for adding new interventions to the enduring body discourse.

Case in point: a few years into his Hollywood career, Alfred Hitchcock was treated to a lengthy *Saturday Evening Post* write-up penned by Alva Johnston. The piece is not remarkable in any sense apart from its pointed attention to Hitchcock's body, which is described in the unflattering detail of the Hitchcockian body discourse. Hitchcock's 300 pounds are advertised in the essay's title, "300-Pound Prophet Comes to Hollywood," followed up by the epithet "the fat director," before the full-figure portrait is reeled in:

Hitchcock's physique made a greater impression on the film capital than his English reputation. Three hundred pounds distributed around five feet, nine inches of height are not to be ignored. The newcomer was a sensation with his cycloramic torso, setting-sun complexions, round, wonderstruck eyes, and cheeks inflated as if blowing an invisible bugle. People reacted to him like children at the sight of balloon giants in Macy's parade.

And the writer continues: "Against the 300-pound background everything relating to Hitchcock attracted attention. He drove about a tiny Austin which fitted him like a bathing suit. He was reported to have the appetite of a lion farm, although, in reality, he is not an immoderate eater."[48] This piece from 1943 echoes the reports from his New York visit in 1937, albeit focusing on the effects of eating rather than eating per se. At

this time the moderate eating in public was distinctly different from his indulgences in private. At the Hitchcocks' Bel-Air mansion the domestic routines gravitated around food preparation: "I designed the kitchen so madame can cook in the most elegant surroundings and serve those of us who patiently wait there, sipping good wine, for her to complete her culinary masterpieces."[49]

The year 1943 was a momentous one weight-wise for Hitchcock. He started out around 300 pounds but embarked on a strenuous dietary regime after the making of *Shadow of a Doubt* that downsized him to slightly above 200 pounds at the end of the year. This achievement was ingeniously outlined in his dual cameo for *Lifeboat* (1944), where his lean incarnation constituted an obverse of the scary sight of himself he encountered the year before. The printed cameo in *Lifeboat* presents Hitchcock in an ad for a dietary cure, Reduco, "the obesity slayer," showing Hitchcock before and after dieting. Reminiscing about his cameos, Hitchcock singled out the one in *Lifeboat* as his favorite. After he appeared in the ad for the fictive weight-loss drug, "letters literally

poured in from fat people, asking where they could buy Reduco, the miracle drug that had helped me lose 100 pounds. Maybe I shouldn't admit it, but I got a certain satisfaction from writing back that the drug didn't exist, and adding smugly that the best way to lose weight was to go on a strenuous diet, as I had done."[50]

Henceforth, dieting became an even more frequent aspect of the reporting on Hitchcock, not least because his weight continued to sharply fluctuate over the years, which sometimes caused unexpected problems. Allardice in an interview jestingly mentioned the difficulties in devising jokes eight weeks ahead not knowing if a new diet would have taken its toll on Hitchcock's body when it was time to shoot the introductions to the television shows. According to a *Newsweek* interview from 1956, Hitch was "down nearly 100 pounds from his top weight of 300—thanks to a diet of steak and no hard liquor." Louella Parsons offered more details concerning the dietary regime a couple of weeks later with photos of Hitch eating and smelling a chicken casserole prepared by Alma. In addition, Hitchcock offered a recipe for steak and kidney pie.[51] In an earlier newspaper discussion of his dieting, readers were invited to request copies for two of his favorite diets: the high-protein diet and the liquid diet.[52]

In the mid-1950s, when Hitchcock began hosting his television show, virtually every appraisal of the show started out with a whack at the host's body—albeit at that time far from spectacularly obese. "One of TV's newest cynosures," *Newsweek* still quipped, "is a penguin-fat man with a pendulous nose, gimlet eyes, and a lower lip like a battered sugar scoop."[53] *Time* had previously set the tone by succinctly headlining its appraisal "The Fat Silhouette."[54] The *New York Herald Tribune* offered a more protracted version:

Mr. Hitchcock, as I suppose everyone now knows, is a man of redoubtable circumference. In fact, he might be described as one of those Englishmen on whom the sun never sets. And he has a face like a slightly malevolent kewpie doll. On his program, the physiognomy and body are first outlined gently in pencil, then inked in. Finally, the man himself floats in, still in darkness. Then they turn the lights on and there he is. CBS, I guess, feels that it would be too great a shock to present the man, cold, without advance preparation, and maybe they're right.[55]

Decades later, when the American Film Institute honored Hitchcock with a lifetime achievement award in 1979, François Truffaut was among the parade of collaborators and colleagues celebrating him. In his speech Truffaut came up with his own version of the importance of being stout to succeed: "When I began to direct films, I thought Monsieur Hitchcock was fantastique, maybe because he weighed more than 200 pounds. Therefore I tried to eat more and more. I gained 20 pounds, but it obviously didn't work. I knew I had to find other ways to touch the proportions of his genius, so I asked Monsieur Hitchcock to give me an interview of 50 hours and to reveal all his secrets. The reason was a book, actually it was like a cookbook, full of recipes for making films."

In an article from the late 1940s, again based on a dinner-table interview in New York City, Mary Morris informed her readers that fat men come in two varieties: "repulsive ones and cute ones." Hitchcock, in her description "fatter than Santa Claus," still exuded the "right amount of charm, wit, and taste" to qualify as one of the cuties. Furthermore, she reflects, he manages to hold the attention of the general public, which "generally doesn't bother to remember the names of movie directors." This obvious cultural capital had its foundation in the body discourse as a prime topic among the talking points Hitchcock had set in motion as soon as he touched down in the United States.[56]

Does the body discourse have any significance outside the sphere of puffery, or did Hitchcock and his team only mobilize his fatness to incessantly keep him in the discursive limelight? In an excellent but seldom mentioned article from 1973, Robert C. Cumbow outlines the contours of a tentative "fat theory" as a biographical foundation for Hitchcock's cinema. Presumably due to lack of space, Cumbow considers neither the television show nor matters of reception in his short piece.[57] Stylistically he notices the centrality of staircases as a recurrent visual motif in Hitchcock's cinema a decade before William Rothman's in-depth analysis of this imagery.[58] Moreover, Cumbow asks, "Why the frequent and deliberate juxtaposition of food images with the discussion of violent death?" Claiming that Hitchcock "deals exclusively in situations of fear and suspense," Cumbow reads this attention resulting from "anxieties and discomforts peculiar to the fat person." Confinement, hydrophobia, and acrophobia are obviously discomforting for fat people, we are told, and in this reading Hitchcock's mastery consists of his brilliant grafting of the fat person's fears onto extremely fit screen characters, which in turn excites in the "viewer of average build a sensation correlative to those which have aroused discomfort and fear in himself as a fat person." Paradigmatic situations in this respect involve entering phone booths and narrow train corridors, or climbing steep stairs—not to mention the physical dexterity required to come out on top in chase scenes, the latter no doubt the bread and butter of Hitchcock's brand of suspense.

For Cumbow the ubiquity of food scenes and their connections to crime—the macabre intersection between dining *à la française* and murder *à l'anglaise*—is related to his claim that "any overweight person has an ambivalent view of food which reaches obsessive proportions." Food is loved and mistrusted and "viewed either with horror or with whimsy." In Hitchcock's cinema, eating and drinking are perennial plot points, "the constant juxtaposition of food with situations involving fear, violence, or death."

Reflecting on Hitchcock's stylistic mastery and consistency, Vincent Canby perceptively invokes the director's voice—fat or not—and notes, "His unheard voice in any movie is as unmistakable as his image that is always seen, though fleetingly."[59] For Cumbow, Hitchcock as obese cameo figure provides virtually the only foil for "the physical attractiveness and ability of his heroes—they endure and accomplish things he can only have nightmares about."

The voice heard by Canby reverberated not only in the segments framing the television dramas but also in the very stories and their stylistic vocabulary—in a highly condensed fashion, given the format and production resources. This Hitchcockian voice is, of course, just another name for a stylistically coherent narrator constructed in the vein of the auteur theory, over which a real but scripted voice hovered as an echo, namely Hitchcock's performance voice that audiences remembered from so many television shows, written in the inimitable style of James Allardice for the "colossus of the macabre."

When Alfred Hitchcock received his first honorary degree, at Santa Clara University, he was enlisted as commencement speaker for the Jesuit institution, located close to Hitchcock's second home and not far from the location of his most recent film, *The Birds*. The citation for the honor named him a "colossus of the macabre" in happy emulation of the double entendres Hitchcock's team excelled in. In his address Hitchcock reciprocated by claiming that the university more than a century ago was founded to produce well-rounded men and reflected, "If I don't qualify as well-round-

ed, I would like to see the man who does." After spending time talking about gravestones and their inscriptions, the importance of humor, God, and matters bearing on life and death, and comparing his own degree to the one conferred on Dr. Jekyll, Hitchcock expressed his gratitude and appreciation of the honor. The wording, once again, illustrates the tenet of this essay: that Hitchcock by way of his television hosting reclaimed the body discourse—set in motion during the gastronomic holiday in New York in 1937—for his own purposes and on his own terms. Still he was trapped in the trappings of his own television image and persona and consequently concluded: "So, when you next see my image flickering on your television screen, if I loom a bit larger, it will not mean I have gained weight—blame it instead on the righteous puff of pride."[60]

# Notes

Preface

**Casting Alfred Hitchcock: An Art Historical Perspective**

DAVID ALAN ROBERTSON

1   Larry Gross, "Parallel Lines: Hitchcock the Screenwriter," *Sight and Sound* (London: British Film Institute, 1999), 38–44.
2   François Truffaut, *Hitchcock,* rev. ed. (New York: Touchstone, 1983).
3   Sidney Gottlieb, ed., *Hitchcock on Hitchcock: Selected Writings and Interviews* (Berkeley and Los Angeles: University of California Press, 1995).
4   "Publicity 1958–1959," folder 544, Alfred Hitchcock Papers, Margaret Herrick Library, Academy of Motion Picture Arts and Sciences (hereafter abbreviated as AMPAS).
5   William E. Wallace, "Michelangelo's Assistants on the Sistine Chapel," *Gazette des Beaux-Arts* 110 (December 1987): 203–16.
6   Wallace, 208.

**1   Creating the Alfred Hitchcock Film: An Introduction**

WILL SCHMENNER

1   Robert Warshow, *The Immediate Experience: Movies, Comics, Theatre and Other Aspects of Popular Culture* (Cambridge, MA, and London: Harvard University Press, 1946), xli.
2   Michael Elias Balcon, "Mr. M. E. Balcon's notes on Thirty Nine Steps," November 26, 1934. Michael Balcon Collection, British Film Institute.
3   *Skin Game* working script (S1441), Document Collection, British Film Institute.
4   André Bazin, "De la politique des auteurs," *Cahiers* 70, April 1957, in *Cahiers du Cinema: The 1950s: Neo-Realism, Hollywood, New Wave,* ed. Jim Hillier (Cambridge, MA: Harvard University Press, 1985), 248.
5   The exhibition is more in line with André Bazin's application of *la politique des auteurs* than with the more hard line *Cahiers* critics. For instance, Bazin emphasized the importance of Gregg Toland's contributions to *Citizen Kane.*
6   Alfred Hitchcock, "Films We Could Make," *London Evening News,* November 16, 1927, in *Hitchcock on Hitchcock: Selected Writings and Interviews,* ed. Sidney Gottlieb (Berkeley and Los Angeles: University of California Press, 1995), 165.
7   In addition to the fluid and constantly refined film canon and *la politique des auteurs*, the rise of the American auteur in the 1970s was one of the driving forces of this cultural shift and perhaps an essential step in the growing case for movies' place in the fine arts museum.
8   Although Hitchcock made strong claims about his ability to visualize, the majority of the time he described it as a process that required time and careful development: "I like to have a film complete in my mind before I go on the floor. Sometimes the first idea one has of a film is of a vague pattern, a sort of haze with a certain shape. There is possibly a colorful opening developing into something more intimate; then, perhaps in the middle, a progression to a chase or some other adventure; and sometimes at the end of the big shape of a climax, or maybe some twist or surprise. You see this hazy pattern, and then you have to find a narrative idea to suit it. Or a story may give you an idea first and you have to develop it into a pattern." Charles Davy, ed., *Footnotes to the Film* (New York: Oxford University Press, 1937), 3–15, reprinted in Gottlieb, 253.
9   Alfred Hitchcock, "Life Among the Stars," *London News Chronicle,* March 1–5, 1937, in Gottlieb, 27.
10  Alfred Hitchcock to Evan Hunter, November 30, 1961, folder 19, Alfred Hitchcock Papers, Margaret Herrick Library, AMPAS.
11  Alfred Hitchcock, "Director's Problems," *The Listener,* February 2, 1938, 241–242 , in Gottlieb, 187.
12  Certainly the Hitchcock movie is not just an idea. A Hitchcock movie tends to have a distinctive visual and thematic style. The idea, however, was important to Hitchcock. He went so far as to say that, "it is ideas we want in films far more than stories. Give us the idea and we can turn you out a story any time." (Hitchcock, "Life Among the Stars," in Gottlieb, 48).
13  Hitchcock, "Life Among the Stars," in Gottlieb, 48.
14  "Mr. Hitchcock's Original Work Copy of *Psycho,* November 10, 1959," folder 566, Alfred Hitchcock Papers, Margaret Herrick Library, AMPAS.
15  Alfred Hitchcock to Sidney L. Bernstein, telegram, October 13, 1948, Sidney L. Bernstein Collection, British Film Institute.
16  Alfred Hitchcock, "Production Methods Compared," *Cine-Technician* 14, no. 75, November–December 1948, 170–174, in Gottlieb, 205.
17  Albert Whitlock, Robert Boyle, Harold Michelson, Richard Edlund, interview by Bill Krohn, Don Shay, Bob Swarthe, Serge LePeron, transcript, *Cahiers du cinéma,* 337 (June 1982), 36–48. English translation by Bill Krohn. Pamphlet files, Margaret Herrick Library, AMPAS.

**2   The Last Word: Images in Hitchcock's Working Method**

SCOTT CURTIS

1   Ian Cameron and V. F. Perkins, "Hitchcock," in *Alfred Hitchcock: Interviews*, ed. Sidney Gottlieb (Jackson, MS: University Press of Mississippi, 2003), 50.
2   Budge Crawley, Fletcher Markle, and Gerald Pratley, "I Wish I Didn't Have to Shoot the Picture: An Interview with Alfred Hitchcock," *Take One* 1, no. 1 (1966): reprinted in Albert J. LaValley, ed., *Focus on Hitchcock* (Englewood Cliffs, NJ: Prentice Hall, 1972), 25.
3   Crawley, Markle, and Pratley, 24.
4   Charles Thomas Samuels, "Alfred Hitchcock," in *Alfred Hitchcock: Interviews,* 133.
5   American Film Institute, "Dialogue on Film: Alfred Hitchcock," in *Alfred Hitchcock: Interviews,* 90.
6   John M. Woodcock, "The Name Dropper: Alfred Hitchcock," in *The American Screenwriter* 40, no. 2 (Summer 1990): 37.
7   Peggy Robertson, interview with Barbara Hall, March 31, 1995, oral history, Margaret Herrick Library, AMPAS.
8   Bill Krohn, *Hitchcock at Work* (London and New York: Phaidon Press, 2000), 84–87.

9 "*Skin Game* working script," S1441, British Film Institute.

10 "Mr. Hitchcock's Original Work Copy of *Psycho*, November 10, 1959," folder 566, Alfred Hitchcock Papers, Margaret Herrick Library, AMPAS.

11 Krohn, 258.

12 "Production—notes & memos, 1962–1963," folder 82, Alfred Hitchcock Papers, Margaret Herrick Library, AMPAS.

13 See, for example, the transcript between Hitchcock, Boyle, and Hunter during the development of *Marnie*, "Script: story outline for production design; 2/4/63," folder 408, Alfred Hitchcock Papers, Margaret Herrick Library, AMPAS. Or the discussion regarding the development of *Stage Fright* between Hitchcock and production manager/producer Fred Aherne, Robert Lennard Collection at the British Film Institute.

14 See Krohn's discussion of Albert Whitlock's troubles and eventual triumph with that shot, *Hitchcock at Work*, 252–255.

15 Hitchcock's script comments to Evan Hunter, November 30, 1961, "Script: script comments; 1961–1962," folder 19, Alfred Hitchcock Papers, Margaret Herrick Library, AMPAS.

16 Hitchcock relates an amusing anecdote about his relationship with writers in one of his interviews: "As for Raymond Chandler, our collaboration [on *Strangers on a Train*] was much less happy. After a while, I had to give up working with him. Sometimes, after we were trying to find ideas for a scene, I would make a suggestion. Instead of seeing whether it might be good, he would remark, with annoyance, 'If you can do this all alone, why the devil do you need me?' He refused all collaboration with the director." Despite Chandler's truculence, and Hitchcock's sometimes coy refusal of credit, this story makes it even clearer that Hitchcock really did need a screenwriter to collaborate with, and not just to come up with dialogue. Rui Nogueira and Nicoletta Zalaffi, "Hitch, Hitch, Hitch, Hurrrah!" in *Alfred Hitchcock: Interviews*, 122.

17 See Dan Auiler, *Hitchcock's Notebooks: An Authorized and Illustrated Look inside the Creative Mind of Alfred Hitchcock* (New York: Spike, 1999), 506.

18 See also Krohn, 52–53.

19 "Production 1956–1958," folder 997, Alfred Hitchcock Papers, Margaret Herrick Library, AMPAS.

20 "Production 1962–1964," folder 473, Alfred Hitchcock Papers, Margaret Herrick Library, AMPAS.

21 "Sketches and notes 1958," folder 550, Alfred Hitchcock Papers, Margaret Herrick Library, AMPAS.

22 Krohn, 206.

23 "Publicity 1958–1959," folder 544, Alfred Hitchcock Papers, Margaret Herrick Library, AMPAS. As far as I can tell, these sketches did not show up in *Coronet* or any other magazine from this period.

### 3 In and Out of the Frame: Paintings in Hitchcock
TOM GUNNING

I would like to thank my friend Will Schmenner, who asked me to write this essay; and Jan Olsson, and Joel Frykolm who helped me write it, with a nod to John Ferguson (Minas Aziloglou).

1 Kerry Brougher and Michael Tarantino, *Notorious: Alfred Hitchcock and Contemporary Art* (Oxford: Museum of Modern Art, 1999); Dominique Païni and Guy Cogeval, *Hitchcock et l'art: coincidences fatale* (Milan: Mazzotta, 2000); Brigitte Peucker, *The Material Image: Art and the Real in Film* (Stanford, CA: Stanford University Press, 2007), 68–103. I would also have to acknowledge the strong influence of the classic works on Hitchcock of Robin Wood, William Rothman, Tania Modeleski, Murray Pomerance, Richard Allen, and others on my approach. However, in contrast to the catalogue essays that deal mainly with the influence of works of art on Hitchcock, or vice versa, my treatment here is more formal and contextual, dealing with painting that appears in Hitchcock's films and whose meaning is defined by their textual roles.

2 Although this certainly overlaps with Peucker's discussion of the relation between "art" and "the real," I think her more psychoanalytical use of the term "the real" differs from my conception of a phenomenal and spatial world of the observer, which does not imply at all the Lacanian concept of the real. Indeed what I call "nothingness" towards the end of this essay seems to me closer to the Lacanian "real," but I try to avoid this frame of reference, preferring a more phenomenological use of these terms. I must add that I find Peucker's use of the Medusa figure especially elegant and revealing.

3 Ben Singer introduced his concept of the "Serial Queen," an active but often victimized heroine frequent in the silent serial films, in his classic essay "Female Power in the Serial-queen Melodrama: the Etiology of an Anomaly." In *Silent Film*, ed. Richard Abel (New Brunswick, NJ: Rutgers University Press, 1996).

4 Laura Mulvey, "Visual Pleasure and Narrative Cinema," in *Visual and Other Pleasures* (Bloomington, IN: University of Indiana Press, 1989).

5 Edgar Allan Poe, "The Oval Portrait," in *Poetry and Tales* (New York: Library of America, 1984), 481–484.

6 On the tradition of "realizing" paintings in *tableaux vivants*, see Myron Meisel, *Realizations: Narrative, Pictorial and Theatrical Arts in Nineteenth-Century England* (Princeton, NJ: Princeton University Press, 1983).

7 Peucker, 78.

8 For early examples of this see "On the Vision of God" in Nicholas Cusanus, *Selected Spiritual Writings* (New York: Paulist Press, 1997), 233–290, and gothic novels from *Varney the Vampire* to *Trilby*.

9 Peucker's analysis of this painting parody as a version of the Medusa and an emergence of the sign of castration seems to me a powerful psychoanalytic reading, especially good in explaining Scottie's reaction. See Peucker, 79–80.

10 I discuss this sequence in my essay "The Desire and Pursuit of the Hole: Cinema's Obscure Object of Desire," *Erotikon*, ed. Shadi Bartech and Thomas Bartescherer (Chicago: University of Chicago Press, 2005), 261–277.

11 Peucker also has a detailed and valuable analysis of these portraits, 75–77.

12 See Paul Ricoeur, *The Symbolism of Evil* (Boston: Beacon Press, 1969), 33–40.

13 Stephen Heath, "Narrative Space," in *Questions of Cinema* (Bloomington: University of Indiana Press, 1981), 19–24.

14 Ibid., 19

15 Ibid., 20.

16 Ibid., 21.

17 Ibid., 24.

18 Peucker is the only critic I know to mention this parallel to the scene from *Suspicion,* 71.

19 André Bazin, "Theater and Cinema," in *What is Cinema?,* vol. 1 (Berkeley, CA: University of California Press, 1967), trans. Hugh Gray, 102.

20 Donald Spoto, *The Dark Side of Genius: The Life of Alfred Hitchcock* (New York: Ballantine Books, 1983), 455.

21 Robert Morris, "Solecisms of Sight: Specular Speculations," in *October* 103 (Winter 2003): 31–41.

22 Ibid., 32.

23 Ibid., 32.

24 Hitchcock does not use a freeze frame in films, except somewhat awkwardly in *Strangers on a Train*, *Topaz*, and perhaps a few other places, where it seems not intended to be noticed.

25 Laura Mulvey, *Death 24x a Second: Stillness and the Moving Image* (London: Reaktion Books, 2006), 101.

## 4  *I Confess* and *Nos deux consciences*
BILL KROHN

1 *Cahiers du cinéma* , April 1957, 40.

2 The Rivette article is cited in Eric Rohmer and Claude Chabrol, *Hitchcock* (Paris: Editions Universitares, 1957), 101. François Truffaut was the first *Cahiers* critic to praise *The Manxman* when it was shown at the Paris Cinémathèque in 1954, comparing it to *I Confess* in his "Petit journal intime du cinéma," *Cahiers du cinéma,* July 1954, 37.

3 Alexandre Astruc, "Au-dessous du volcan," *Cahiers du cinéma,* April 1951, 32.

4 Maurice Scherer, "De trois films et d'une certaine école," *Cahiers du cinéma,* August–September 1953, 18–25.

5 Jean-Luc Godard, "Le cinéma et son double," *Cahiers du cinéma*, June 1957, 40.

6 Rohmer and Chabrol, 158.

7 André Bazin, "Hitchcock contre Hitchcock," *Cahiers du cinéma,* October 1954, 31.

8 Rohmer and Chabrol, 106.

9 Jacques Rivette, "L'art de la fugue," *Cahiers du cinéma,* August–September 1953, 49–52.

10 John Russell Taylor, *Hitch: The Life and Times of Alfred Hitchcock* (New York: Pantheon Books, 1978), 221, and Stephen White, who has Verneuil's records of his labyrinthine negotiations with Hitchcock (private communication): "In November 1946, Verneuil pitched the idea to him…. Verneuil withdrew his complaint from the Writer's Guild and settled with Hitchcock on August 4, 1947." On Verneuil's authority, White believes that Hitchcock first heard of the play from Verneuil because there was not an English translation or, ipso facto, any English production of *Nos deux consciences* that Hitchcock could have seen in the 1930s. But Hitchcock could have seen or read the play during one of his visits to Paris in the early 1930s. (Ken Mogg informs me that there is a French edition of the play in the Library of Congress.) The Truffaut interview makes it sound as if Hitchcock actually heard the story first from Verneuil, but when Bazin referred to Verneuil's "furnishing" the play to him four years earlier, Hitchcock amended: "Sold it" (see Bazin). This would not have kept him from letting Verneuil believe that he was hearing about the idea for the first time when the agent pitched it, just as he did when Bazin explained transference of guilt to him in 1954. He would probably not have told him, at the outset of protracted and very tough negotiations, that he had been haunted for more than a decade by the play he was trying to purchase, any more than he would have admitted this to Truffaut, who had just described *Nos deux consciences* as "a mediocre play": François Truffaut, *Hitchcock* (New York: Touchstone, 1984), 199.

11 Rohmer and Chabrol, 41.

12 Rohmer and Chabrol, 49.

13 Eric Rohmer, "Le soupçon," *Cahiers du cinéma,* May 1952, 64.

14 Rohmer and Chabrol, 105.

15 Rohmer and Chabrol, 49.

16 Rohmer and Chabrol, 78.

17 Rohmer and Chabrol, 88.

18 Rohmer and Chabrol, 84–85.

19 Rohmer and Chabrol, 91.

20 Rohmer and Chabrol, 96.

21 Patrick McGilligan, *Alfred Hitchcock: A Life in Darkness and Light* (New York: Regan Books, 2003), 401.

22 Preface, *Les membres de la commune et du Comité Central,* Paul Delion [i.e. Paul Bourde] (Paris: A. Lemerre, 1871).

23 Murray Pomerance, *An Eye for Hitchcock* (New Brunswick, NJ: Rutgers University Press, 2004), 173.

24 Translation: "Now *that's* cinema!" Caroline Moorhead, *Sidney Bernstein: A Biography* (London: J. Cape, 1984), 183.

25 McGilligan, 441.

26 Helen Simpson, *Under Capricorn* (London: W. Heinemann, 1937), 114.

## 5  Hitchcock à la Carte: Menus, Marketing, and the Macabre
JAN OLSSON

1 Budge Crawley, Fletcher Markle, and Gerald Pratley, "I Wish I Didn't Have to Shoot the Picture: An Interview with Alfred Hitchcock," *Take One* 1, no. 1 (1966); reprinted in Albert J. LaValley, ed. *Focus on Hitchcock.* (Englewood Cliffs, NJ: Prentice Hall, 1972).

2 For a detailed description of the opening sequence, see Robert E. Kapsis, *Hitchcock: The Making of a Reputation* (Chicago: University of Chicago Press, 1992), 31.

3 The corpus of Alfred Hitchcock's films and television programs is indeed rich: 23 films in Britain from 1925 to 1938; 30 features in the United States from 1939 to 1976; more than 370 television shows hosted, of which he directed 20, plus an avalanche of publishing endeavors in his name, mystery magazines, crime anthologies, vinyl recordings, board games, etc.

4 Cary Wetterau, "Celebrity Parade," *Miami Herald,* February 1, 1958. Hitchcock's Florida adventure was launched just prior to the airing of "Heartbeat," produced for NBC's *Suspicion*.

5 Walter Ames, "Hitchcock Tosses Luncheon Party…in Beverly Hills Jail," *Los Angeles Times*, September 26, 1956. The event was orchestrated shortly before the second season of *Alfred Hitchcock Presents* opened.

6 See Kapsis on Leonard J. Leff, *Hitchcock & Selznick* (New York: Weidenfeld & Nicolson, 1987).

7 Jerry Tallmer, "The Unflappable Hitch," *New York Post,* July 15, 1972.

8 For the trajectory of Hitchcock's critical standing, see Kapsis, 1992.

9 Bosley Crowther, "Screen: '*The Trouble with Harry* ': Whimsical Film from Hitchcock at Paris," *New York Times,* October 18, 1955.

10 John Crosby, "Macabre Merriment," *New York Herald Tribune,* November 16, 1955, reprinted in LaValley, 138. Similar assessments were repeatedly ventured by Cecil Smith in the *Los Angeles Times,* for example: "The macabre little tales of the Sunday night series, however, have been a TV staple, enormously popular with viewers. I've suspected, however, that it is Mr. Hitchcock's own inimitable presence leading into the shows and his gentle method of poking fun at the grimmest of stories that has brought about the popularity." "Chill Master Hitchcock to do Thriller No. 100," *Los Angeles Times,* March 1, 1958. Or, "It has always seemed to me that the success of Alfred Hitchcock's Sunday evening shocking playlets is based primarily on Mr. Hitchcock's own pixie appearances, which give the laugh to the whole thing. No matter how grisly the subject matter, and he has dealt with cannibalism among other unsavory matter—his rotund figure before and after the story always seems to indicate that this has been so much poppycock and he is pulling your leg." Cecil Smith, "Hitch Turn Off Relieving Humor," *Los Angeles Times,* April 5, 1960.

11 His culinary preferences were very precise, and according to a French interview there was only one kitchen of merit. "Seulment la cuisine française. Les autres n'existent pas. Je n'aime d'ailleurs que les plates simples… mais bons. Et sans sauce, évidement." Anonymous, "Hitchcock vous dit la vérité sur Hitchcock," *Télé-Magazine* 5, no. 210 (November 1959), 1–7. Later, when Hitchcock was invited to Paris, the "French Film Society Secretary Henri Langlois made Hitchcock an honorary Frenchman because, 'You know how to drink well and eat well.'" Anonymous, "Body has a Voice—If Anyone Cares," *Los Angeles Times,* January 15, 1971.

12 Ads in several newspapers on March 26; comments on the quest in Meyer Berger, "Quest for Haunted House Here Finds Ghosts Shun Metropolis Steel and Concrete," *New York Times,* February 29, 1956. Hy Gardner, "Coast to Coast," *New York Herald Tribune,* February 27, 1956.

13 Meyer Berger, "Haunted-House Party Plans a Macabre Menu," *New York Times,* March 5, 1956.

14 Robert H. Prall, "Spooks Ready for Hitchcock Party," *New York World-Telegram and Sun,* March 7, 1956; Robert H. Prall, "Hitchcock Honors Ghosts with Loving Ghoulishness," *New York World-Telegram and Sun,* March 8, 1956.

15 Donald Spoto, *The Dark Side of Genius: The Life of Alfred Hitchcock* (New York: Ballantine Books, 1984), 407–8.

16 The selecting of stories for the television shows was predicated on a form of obliqueness, namely a twist ending or turnaround plot device. In a rare letter to one of his story scouts, Hitchcock describes what he was looking for, namely "short stories by well-known authors…definitely of the suspense, or thriller, type…one important factor that should be common to all of them, and i[s] that the ending should have a 'twist' almost to a point of shock in either the last line or the last situation." Letter to Mary Elson, February 24, 1955, Alfred Hitchcock Papers, Margaret Herrick Library, AMPAS.

17 Anonymous, "Murders in U.S. Lack Charm, Says Expert," *New York Sunday News,* October 26, 1958.

18 Alfred Hitchcock, "My Recipe for Murder," *Coronet* 48, no. 5 (September, 1960): 49–61.

19 Gregg Kilday, "Hitchcock's Triumph of Tension," *Los Angeles Times,* July 27, 1975. For elaborations on the old-world charm of murders, see Alfred Hitchcock, "Murder—With English on It," *New York Times,* March 3, 1957; *Washington Post,* June 11, 1972; and Anonymous, "Conversation with Alfred Hitchcock," *Oui,* February 1973, 82–114.

20 Rex Reed, "Oh, What a Lovely Murder," *Washington Post,* June 11, 1972.

21 Anonymous, "Hitchcock Gives Free Rein to THE GENTLE SEX," *TV Guide,* May 10–16, 1958, 12–13.

22 Richard Schickel, "We're Living in a Hitchcock World, All Right," *New York Times,* October 29, 1972.

23 Thomas M. Leitch, *Find the Director and Other Hitchcock Games* (Athens: University of Georgia Press, 1991).

24 "After-Dinner Speech at the Screen Producers Guild Dinner," reprinted in Sidney Gottlieb, ed., *Hitchcock on Hitchcock. Selected Writings and Interviews* (Berkeley and Los Angeles: University of California Press, 1995), 186–187, 55–56.

25 Paul Speegle, "Hitchcock up to His Second Chin in Art," *San Francisco Chronicle,* August 27, 1939.

26 "Old Ruts Are New Ruts [1938]," reprinted in Gottlieb, *Hitchcock on Hitchcock,* 202.

27 H. Allen Smith, "Hitchcock Likes to Smash Cups," *New York World-Telegram,* August 28, 1937.

28 Janet White, "Picture Parade," *Brooklyn Daily Eagle,* August 30, 1937.

29 Anonymous, "Falstaff in Manhattan: Alfred Hitchcock Tests Our Kitchens and Our Taste in Melodrama," *New York Times,* September 5, 1937.

30 Anonymous, "Entertainment," *Newsweek,* October 17, 1938, 28–29.

31 Anonymous, "Hitchcock 'Cuts' Tea for T-Bone," *New York Morning Telegraph,* August 26, 1937, 2; Anonymous, "Arrived," *Newsweek,* September 6, 1937, 25.

32 Archer Winsten, "Movie Talk," *New York Post,* August 27, 1937.

33 Irving Hoffman, "Tales of Hoffman," *Hollywood Reporter,* August 30, 1937. Hitchcock was at the time working for Gaumont-British.

34 Eileen Creelman, "Picture Plays and Players," *New York Sun,* June 15, 1938.

35 B. R. Crisler, "Hitchcock: Master Melodramatist," *New York Times,* June 12, 1938.

36 Anonymous, "News of the Studios," *New York Sun,* March 6, 1939.

37 Leonard Lyons, "No Steak and Ice Cream," *New York Post,* August 23, 1943.

38 Hitchcock Clippings, 1950s folder, Performing Arts Library, New York; also in Alfred Hitchcock Papers, Margaret Herrick Library, AMPAS.

39 Bill Davidson, "Alfred Hitchcock Resents," *Saturday Evening Post,* December 15, 1962, 62–64.

40 Oriana Fallaci, "Alfred Hitchcock: Mr. Chastity [1963]," reprinted in Sidney Gottlieb, ed., *Alfred Hitchcock Interviews* (Jackson, MS: University Press of Mississippi, 2003), 60.

41 The obituary in the *Chicago Tribune* emphasizes how the trappings of the television shows became "immediately identifiable trademarks," namely "his profile, his caustic and ghoulish remarks about life and commercials, and theme song." Anonymous, "Suspense Master Alfred Hitchcock Dies," April 30, 1980. Peter B. Flint arrived at a more or less similar assessment: "He became somewhat of a national institution in shaping a public image as genially ghoulish cynic noted for barbed pronouncements about life and commercials in two popular weekly television series." "Alfred Hitchcock Dies," *New York Times,* April 30, 1980.

42 Spoto, 376.

43  Alfred Hitchcock, ed., *Alfred Hitchcock Presents: Stories They Wouldn't Let Me Do on Television* (New York: Simon and Schuster, 1957), viii.

44  Alfred Hitchcock, "Sixty Minutes Next Season," *Morning Telegraph,* August 21, 1962. See Hitchcock Clippings, at the Performing Arts Library, New York.

45  Walter Wanger, "Hollywood Genius," *Current History and Forum* 52, no. 6 (December 24, 1940): 13.

46  L.B., "The Complete Hitchcock," *Los Angeles Times,* June 3, 1951.

47  Geoffrey T. Hellmann, "Alfred Hitchcock: England's Best and Biggest Director Goes to Hollywood," *Life* (November 20, 1939): 39.

48  Alva Johnston, "300-Pound Prophet Comes to Hollywood," *Saturday Evening Post* (May 22, 1943). Some formulations echo Russell Maloney's portrait in the *New Yorker,* September 10, 1938, 24–28; for example, "Spiritually and physically, he might be akin to a Macy balloon." Maloney refers to the "steak-and-ice-cream" regime as a canard, which Smith's eyewitness report from Club 21 does not support. According to Maloney, Hitchcock at the time was on a diet and had lost 25 out of 290 pounds .

49  Bill Davidson, 64. For photographic documentation of the Hitchcocks' humble abode in Bel-Air, albeit without an image from the kitchen, see Anonymous, "Hitchcock Brews Thrillers Here," *House and Garden* 82 (August 1942): 34–35.

50  Alfred Hitchcock, "The Role I Liked Best…," *Saturday Evening Post,* December 2, 1950, 138. Hitchcock elaborated on his dietary regime in an interview conducted at St. Regis while "thumbing through a tattered little yellow volume entitled *Pocket Guide to Calorie Counting.*" The reporter who arrived at the hotel doubting the reports on the director's recent weight loss prior to *Lifeboat* was "determined to interview a *fat* Alfred Hitchcock." Somewhat disappointed, the anonymous reporter encountered "this sturdy, youngish man with big eyes in a bland face, looking positively thin to us," a fact ingeniously headlined in the write-up. Anonymous, "The Man Who Weighed Too Much," *Cue* 12 (December 18, 1943): 10.

51  Louella O. Parsons, "Kitchen No Mystery to the Master of Mystery," *Los Angeles Examiner,* June 24, 1956, magazine section, n.p.; Anonymous, "Alfred Hitchcock: Director," *Newsweek,* June 11, 1956: 105–108; see also Paul Foster, "Alfred Hitchcock—An Expert in Tension," *Sketch* 223 (November 2, 1955): 451, for yet another discussion of weight loss and diets.

52  Lydia Lane, "It's Time Now to Start Taking Off That Turkey and Eggnog Waistline," *Los Angeles Times,* January 18, 1955.

53  Anonymous, "Alfred Hitchcock: Director," *Newsweek,* June 11, 1956, 105.

54  Anonymous, "The Fat Silhouette," *Time,* December 26, 1955, 46.

55  John Crosby, "Macabre Merriment," *New York Herald Tribune,* November 16, 1955, reprinted in LaValley, 138.

56  Mary Morris, item from the latter half of the 1940s without date and source indication in Hitchcock Clippings at the Performing Arts Library, New York.

57  Robert C. Cumbow, "Of Staircases and Potato Trucks: Fear and Fatness and Alfred Hitchcock," *Movietone News,* no. 25 (September 1973): 612. In Michael Walker's recent book *Hitchcock's Motifs* (Amsterdam: Amsterdam University Press, 2005), one section is devoted to food, and a subsection discusses Hitchcock's famous aversion to eggs. Apart from Walker's charting of Hitchcock's cinematic menus, David Greven has dissected the eating habits in a group of Hitchcock films in "Engorged with Desire: The Films of Alfred Hitchcock and the Gendered Politics of Eating," in Anne L. Bower, ed., *Reel Food: Essays on Food and Film* (New York: Routledge, 2004): 297–310.

58  William Rothman, *Hitchcock: The Murderous Gaze* (Cambridge, MA, and London: Harvard University Press, 1982), 33 and passim.

59  Vincent Canby, "Film Maker Transformed Commonplace into Exotic," *New York Times*, April 30, 1980.

60  The commencement address was published in the *Santa Claran,* summer 1963.

# PLATES

# Introduction to Plates

Drawings, sketches, storyboards, and documentation, now located in archives in England and the United States, give us a sense of how Hitchcock's movies came together and how he carefully shepherded the collective vision of his movies from conception to the theater. Reproduced in this section are approximately a third of the objects from the exhibition, many of which are undated and untitled (although titles have been created for the catalogue and exhibition). All derive from preproduction or production phases—either before or during filming—of a Hitchcock movie. The preproduction phase was detailed and extensive for all of Hitchcock's projects.

During the course of preproduction and production, Hitchcock constantly revisualized his movies. In general, Hitchcock began with a story or idea, however short, and worked quickly to develop a look for the film. Each step in the process often included a conversation with his department heads, leading to the creation of many of the objects shown here—among them, costume design drawings, production design sketches, set designs, visual effects diagrams, written scene descriptions, shot lists, storyboards, and camera angle drawings. Hitchcock's collaborators usually took one of the director's suggestions and expanded upon it, thereby making a collectively created object that integrated their ideas.

In this spirit, the plates are meant to correspond roughly to the steps Hitchcock may have taken with his collaborators. They follow a loose chronology, working from general decisions about the look of a film to specific decisions about a given scene to actual shooting storyboards to, finally, the apparatus of publicity. It is a loose chronology because many of the decisions made during the course of filmmaking do not follow a particular order. For example, costume design can precede or follow storyboards, and dialogue can be written on the set. Indeed, part of Hitchcock's genius was his ability to synthesize the work of his collaborators. Because the plates pull together the widest possible variety of objects from the breadth of Hitchcock's career, they do not trace any one movie from beginning to end. Instead, the exhibition and the plates take the objects that are extant and available and present them as a collage of how a typical Hitchcock film was created.

Ultimately, the objects challenge our predominant conception of the relationship between art and authorship. Hitchcock's movies were his vision, but his vision was a collective one—a vision that was shared by the director and his collaborators through their discussions and the objects they created.

Before beginning work on the script of *The Birds*, Alfred Hitchcock sent Daphne du Maurier's novella to production designer Robert Boyle. These drawings (plate 1) were the beginning of what would be a long conversation about the film's production design and Boyle's visual response to the story. Although the colors ultimately were not nearly as dark as Boyle's depictions, the eerie foreboding expressed in these sketches resonates through subsequent sketches and the completed film.

The costume design department often operated with more independence than any other department. Whether led by Irene Saltern (plate 2) or Edith Head (plate 4), the department created full color sketches usually based only on general descriptions of the types of clothes Hitchcock wanted for a character—for example, an evening dress or a suit and hat.

1 **Robert Boyle** (American, born 1909)
Production design, *The Birds, Preliminary Sketches*, 1963
Graphite, watercolor, and gouache on paper
21 x 27-1/2 inches
Robert Boyle Papers, Margaret Herrick Library,
Academy of Motion Picture Arts and Sciences. Courtesy
of Universal Studios Licensing LLLP.

'THE BIRDS'
AN
ALFRED. HITCHCOCK. PROD.
PRELIMINARY SKETCHES
BY
ROBERT BOYLE. PROD. DESIGNER
FROM
THE NOVELLA
BY
DAPHNE DUMAURIER

*Fitted coat of imported Duchaine woolen in rose-beige and brown with clever arrangement of sables. Attached in front around the yoke they hang free in back to be casually draped over arms.*

*Priscilla Lane
in "Saboteur"
Alfred Hitchcock Picture
for Universal*

2  **Irene Saltern** (American, 1911–2005)
Costume design, *Priscilla Lane in Saboteur*, 1942
Graphite and gouache on illustration board
20 x 15 inches
Leonard Stanley Collection, Margaret Herrick
Library, Academy of Motion Picture Arts
and Sciences. Courtesy of Universal Studios
Licensing LLLP.

3  **Roger Furse** (British, 1903–1972)
Costume design, *Stage Fright, Costume for
Miss Jane Wyman*, 1950
Graphite and watercolor on paper
17 x 13 inches
British Film Institute, Stills, Posters, and Designs,
17246.

4  **Richard J. Hopper** (American, 1931–1992), illustrator
and **Edith Head** (American, 1897–1981), costume
design
Costume design, *Grace Kelly in To Catch a Thief*, 1955
Ink and watercolor on paper
17-3/4 x 11-3/4 inches
British Film Institute, Stills, Posters, and Designs, 445.
Courtesy of Paramount Pictures.

"Stage Fright"
Costume for
Miss Jane Wyman

Grace Kelly
Bar. Sequence
and Hotel
corridor –

shades soft blue
chiffon –
(blue violet)

When Hitchcock was making films, there were studio art departments staffed by highly talented illustrators and designers. Their sketches for set designs often included suggestions for blocking, camera angles, and lighting—suggestions that technically fell outside the department's purview. The nature of illustrative drawing entailed interpretation and visualization of the scene as well. It is impossible to depict a set without conveying elements of the mise-en-scène.

The ominous lighting in Ray Simm's sketch from *The 39 Steps* (plate 6) and the dynamic character movements and extreme perspectives in Tom Morahan's sketches for *Jamaica Inn* (plates 7 and 8) are examples of how art department drawings did not simply address an isolated aspect of film production. While some of these suggestions were not incorporated, the drawings consistently established a look for the spaces created for the film and initiated a dialogue about its overall tone.

5  **Alfred Junge** (German, 1886–1964)
Production design for *Young and Innocent*, 1937
Charcoal and watercolor on paper
22 x 30-1/4 inches
British Film Institute, Stills, Posters, and Designs, 139.
Copyright: ITV PLC (Granada Int'l)/LFI.

6  **Ray Simm**  (biography unknown)
Production design for *The 39 Steps*, 1935
Graphite and watercolor on paper
15 x 17-3/4 inches
British Film Institute, Stills, Posters, and Designs, 440.
Copyright: ITV PLC (Granada Int'l)/LFI.

7   **Tom Morahan** (British, 1906–1969)
    Production design for *Jamaica Inn*, 1939
    Charcoal and watercolor on paper
    13-3/4 x 19-3/4 inches
    British Film Institute, Stills, Posters, and Designs, 447.
    Copyright: ITV PLC (Granada Int'l) / LFI.

8   **Tom Morahan** (British, 1906–1969)
    Production design for *Jamaica Inn*, 1939
    Charcoal and watercolor on paper
    17-1/4 x 19-3/4 inches
    British Film Institute, Stills, Posters, and Designs, 448.
    Copyright: ITV PLC (Granada Int'l) / LFI.

9 Unknown illustrator and **Alexander Golitzen**
(American, 1908–2005), production designer
Production design for *Foreign Correspondent*, 1940
Watercolor on illustration board
22 x 30 inches
Robert Boyle Papers, Margaret Herrick Library,
Academy of Motion Picture Arts and Sciences.
Courtesy of the Caidin Trust.

10  **James Basevi** (British, 1890–1962)
Production design for *Spellbound*, 1945
Charcoal and watercolor on paper
12-1/4 x 16-1/2 inches
Courtesy of the British Film Institute, Stills,
Posters, and Designs, 12786.
Courtesy of Disney.

Plates 11 and 12 illustrate visual effects. Plate 11 reproduces a gouache rendering of the gas station and restaurant in Bodega Bay, the setting of *The Birds*. A clear plastic sheet, upon which Albert Whitlock painted 13 birds, is placed over the illustration board. As a whole the painting and overlay represent the visual effect: the birds were filmed separately and overlaid upon the shot of the gas station, creating the illusion of an attack.

Plate 12 is a study for a matte for *Marnie*. A matte shot is a commonly used technique in which two images are combined into one. This technique gives filmmakers an array of options, allowing them to insert, even on location shoots, objects and settings that are not actually there. In this study everything above the red line will be integrated into the final image later, including the very top of the house's roof, the sky, and most of the barn.

11  **Albert Whitlock** (British, 1915–1999)
Production design and visual effect study for *The Birds*, 1963
Gouache on clear plastic over gouache on illustration board
15 x 23 inches
Robert Boyle Papers, Margaret Herrick Library, Academy
of Motion Picture Arts and Sciences. Courtesy of Universal
Studios Licensing LLLP.

12  Unknown illustrator and **Robert Boyle** (American,
born 1909), production designer
Production design, *Study for matte* for *Marnie*, 1964
Felt tip marker and colored pencil on illustration board
20 x 30-1/4 inches
Robert Boyle Papers, Margaret Herrick Library, Academy
of Motion Picture Arts and Sciences. Courtesy of Universal
Studios Licensing LLLP.

Plates 13 and 14, drawn by Hitchcock, represent early sketches of the final action sequence in *Saboteur* on and around the torch of the Statue of Liberty. Both drawings show the fall of saboteur Frank Fry (Norman Lloyd) over the torch's railing. The action of the fall itself is represented by drawing Fry multiple times. When this sequence was ultimately filmed, however, Fry fell off the opposite side of the torch. These sketches were also used to begin designing the large scale model of the torch that was constructed in the studio for the stunt scenes.

Plate 15 is a set of designs for the Mount Rushmore House in *North by Northwest*. Hitchcock had instructed production designer Robert Boyle to design a house that Cary Grant could easily climb. In response Boyle drafted the Frank Lloyd Wright-inspired Mount Rushmore House—one of the more memorable sets in film history. He drew these studies in his New York City hotel while scouting locations for the film.

**13  Alfred Hitchcock** (British, 1899–1980)
Sketch for *Saboteur*, 1942
Graphite on paper mounted on board
11-1/2 x 9 inches
Robert Boyle Papers, Margaret Herrick Library,
Academy of Motion Picture Arts and Sciences.
Courtesy of Universal Studios Licensing LLLP.

**14  Alfred Hitchcock** (British, 1899–1980)
Sketch for *Saboteur*, 1942
Graphite on paper
9-1/2 x 8 inches
Robert Boyle Papers, Margaret Herrick Library,
Academy of Motion Picture Arts and Sciences.
Courtesy of Universal Studios Licensing LLLP.

**15  Robert Boyle** (American, born 1909)
Production design, *North by Northwest, Studies for the Mt. Rushmore House*, 1959
Ink and graphite on tracing paper mounted on illustration board
20-1/4 x 30-1/4 inches
Robert Boyle Papers, Margaret Herrick Library,
Academy of Motion Picture Arts and Sciences.
NORTH BY NORTHWEST © Turner Entertainment Co.
A Warner Bros. Entertainment Company.
All Rights Reserved.

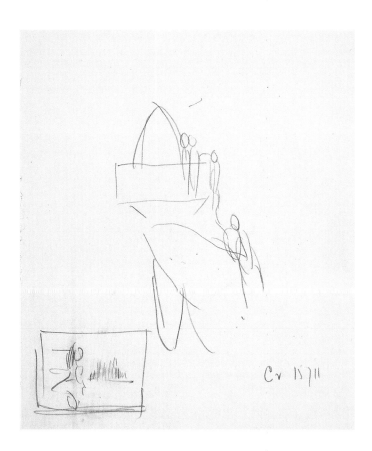

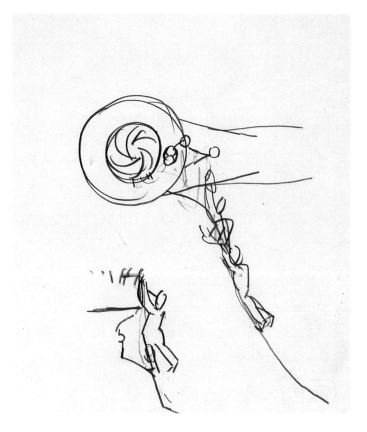

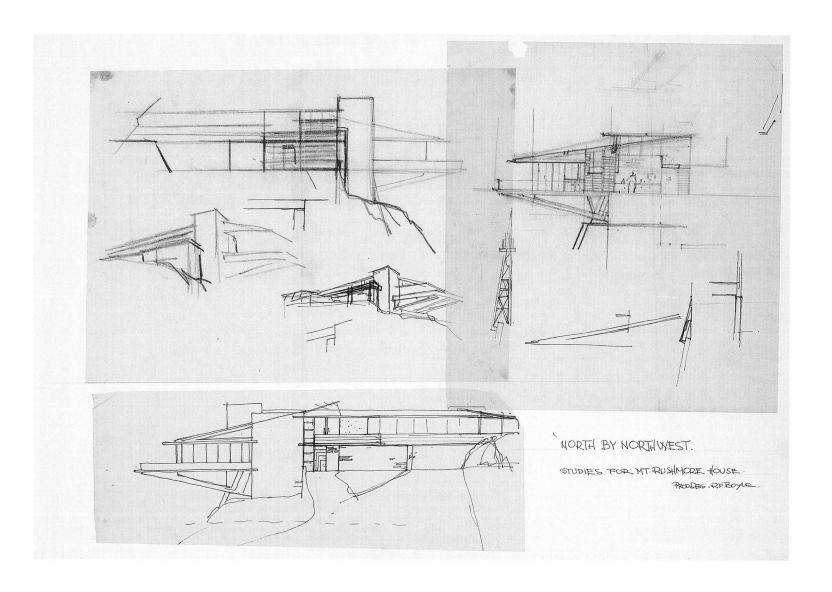

NORTH BY NORTHWEST.

STUDIES FOR MT. RUSHMORE HOUSE.

PROD.DES. R.F.BOYLE.

In this telegram to Hitchcock (plate 17), Kay Brown, a Hollywood agent, suggests several writers for the movie that would become *Shadow of a Doubt*. Brown tries to steer Hitchcock away from noted playwright Thornton Wilder, about whom Hitchcock had inquired, her "first choice" being screenwriter Paul Osborn. And as usual with Hitchcock's collaborators she is happy to suggest many alternatives, especially since any of these writers, including Wilder, could already have been signed to studio contracts.

Perhaps because Hitchcock was lucky or perhaps because of his reputation for quality work, Wilder was available and interested. Two days later, via a telegram to producer Jack Skirball (plate 16), Wilder indicated he wanted "to work with Mr. Hitchcock on the plotting of the dramatic interest." He would primarily develop the film's characters and outline its plot. After Wilder worked on the script, Sally Benson was brought in to polish the dialogue and add a lighter touch. Both understood from the beginning that their contribution would entail collaborating with, rather than simply working for, Hitchcock. In fact, Wilder, who had enlisted in the Psychological Warfare Division of the United States Army, wrote the last pages of his draft on the way to his military assignment in Florida, accompanied on the train by Hitchcock.

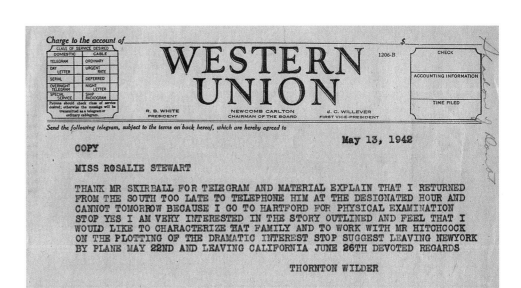

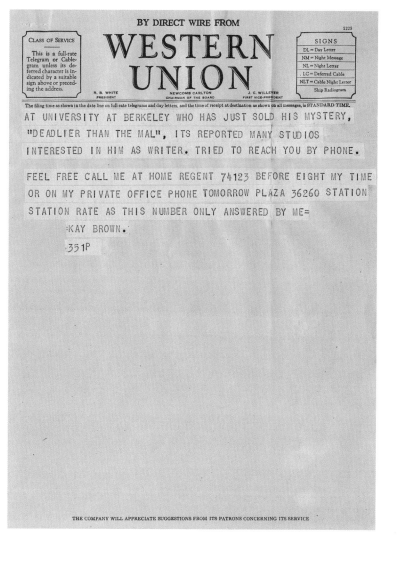

**BY DIRECT WIRE FROM**

**WESTERN UNION**

| CLASS OF SERVICE | | SIGNS |
|---|---|---|
| This is a full-rate Telegram or Cablegram unless its deferred character is indicated by a suitable sign above or preceding the address. | | DL = Day Letter |
| | | NM = Night Message |
| | | NL = Night Letter |
| | | LC = Deferred Cable |
| | | NLT = Cable Night Letter |
| R. B. WHITE PRESIDENT | NEWCOMB CARLTON CHAIRMAN OF THE BOARD    J. C. WILLEVER FIRST VICE-PRESIDENT | Ship Radiogram |

The filing time as shown in the date line on full-rate telegrams and day letters, and the time of receipt at destination as shown on all messages, is STANDARD TIME.

SJ165 TWS PAID 4=NEWYORK NY MAY 11 532P

ALFRED HITCHCOCK=

    CARE UNIVERSAL STUDIOS   OR TRY 601 STCLOUD AVE

    BELAIR BEVERLYHILLS CALIF=

FIRST CHOICE IS PAUL OSBORN WHO I UNDERSTAND FINISHING
ASSIGNMENT AT MGM. OTHER CHOICES, THE HACKETTS, CECIL HOLM.
THORNTON WILDER IN WASHINGTON AND WONT KNOW HIS AVAILABILITY
UNTIL TOMORROW. THOMAS JOB, ALTHOUGH ENGLISH HAS LIVED HERE
SO LONG, COMPLETELY FAMILIAR AMERICAN SCENE, AVAILABLE AFTER

20TH DATE OF HIS OPENING NEW PLAY "UNCLE HARRY". WHAT ABOUT
THE LOCKRIDGES AUTHORS OF MR MRS NORTH? SECOND STRING
DRAMATISTS AVAILABLE:

    KENYON NICHOLSON, CHARLOTTE ARMSTRONG WHO JUST
WROTE JANE COWL PLAY WHICH UNFORTUNATELY FLOPPED OUT OF TOWN,
SHE ALSO MYSTERY STORY WRITER. ROBERT ARDWAY AVAILABLE IN
HOLLYWOOD. OTHER SUGGESTIONS ARE NOVELISTS: MARITTA WOLFF

AUTHOR "WHISTLE STOP"....STOP", MAUREEN DALY AUTHOR
"SEVENTEENTH SUMMER." RUTH MCKINNEY IMMEDIATELY AVAILABLE
AS NEW NOVEL JUST COMPLETED. WRITING TEAM OF RICHARD WEBB
AND HUGH WHEELER WHO PUBLISH MYSTERIES UNDER NAMES OF Q.
PATRICK, PATRIC QUENTIN AND JONATHAN STAGG. STOP. DOROTHY
DISNEY. GRACE WARING STONE. DO YOU KNOW JIMMY GUNN SENIOR

THE COMPANY WILL APPRECIATE SUGGESTIONS FROM ITS PATRONS

---

**BY DIRECT WIRE FROM**

**WESTERN UNION**

AT UNIVERSITY AT BERKELEY WHO HAS JUST SOLD HIS MYSTERY,
"DEADLIER THAN THE MAL", ITS REPORTED MANY STUDIOS
INTERESTED IN HIM AS WRITER. TRIED TO REACH YOU BY PHONE.

FEEL FREE CALL ME AT HOME REGENT 74123 BEFORE EIGHT MY TIME
OR ON MY PRIVATE OFFICE PHONE TOMORROW PLAZA 36260 STATION
STATION RATE AS THIS NUMBER ONLY ANSWERED BY ME=

    KAY BROWN.

    351P

THE COMPANY WILL APPRECIATE SUGGESTIONS FROM ITS PATRONS CONCERNING ITS SERVICE

---

16  **Thornton Wilder** (American, 1897–1975)
Telegram to Rosalie Stewart regarding *Shadow of a Doubt*, May 13, 1942
Alfred Hitchcock Papers, Margaret Herrick Library,
Academy of Motion Picture Arts and Sciences.
Courtesy of Universal Studios Licensing LLLP.

17  **Kay Brown** (American, 1903–1995)
Telegram to Alfred Hitchcock regarding *Shadow of a Doubt*, May 11, 1942
Alfred Hitchcock Papers, Margaret Herrick Library,
Academy of Motion Picture Arts and Sciences.
Courtesy of Universal Studios Licensing LLLP.

During the preproduction of *Marnie*, Hitchcock elaborated upon his outline for the film with an impromptu sketch. Plate 18 shows page seven of an outline Hitchcock and scriptwriter Evan Hunter had completed. Plate 19 is a drawing in Hitchcock's hand on the back of the outline. When the outline was written, the Rutland Robbery—plot outline number 22—had only been named; it had not yet been described. In his drawing, however, Hitchcock visualized the scene nearly as it would be shot.

In this sequence the title character (Tippi Hedren) is burglarizing a company's safe. A cleaning lady approaches the office—she is near the second set of desks, represented by the small rectangles. Someone from the hallway next to the stairs is also approaching. The two angles illustrate the camera angles for the two shots Hitchcock envisioned for this scene. Although he changed the camera placement slightly, this drawing is remarkably close to the sequence as it appeared in *Marnie* and is a prime example of Hitchcock's ability to visualize.

While reviewing a draft of the *Torn Curtain* script, Hitchcock drew two sketches of a scene and inserted them into the bound script. Scene 142 is a description of Professor Michael Armstrong (Paul Newman) falling down the stairs (plate 20). The first sketch is of Armstrong and three other characters approaching the next flight of stairs (plate 21). When filmed the scene was flipped from left to right. The second sketch is of Armstrong's fall. The script describes an action that cannot be captured by a motion picture camera; the camera cannot "retreat holding him in close" while Armstrong tumbles down the stairs. In Hitchcock's revisualization he simplified the shot. Instead of having an impractical tracking shot of Armstrong tumbling down the stairs, Hitchcock drew a close-up of Armstrong falling that he later shot with rear projection.

18) __THE LIGHTNING SCENE__ (cont'd)

Almost as now written, but strengthen red herring that Marnie is responding to Mark's approach, and have her accept invitation to racetrack.

19) __THE RACETRACK SCENE__

Almost as now written, but indicate that Marnie is frightened by "Haven't I seen you before?" because she is falling for Mark and does not want him to know of her past. Mark asks her to dinner with his mother on Tuesday night, and she accepts.

20) __THE TUESDAY NIGHT DATE__

Where we meet Mark's mother, gracious, dignified, gentle, and warm, for the first time. It is apparent that she takes to Marnie at once. In a scene with the two women alone, she talks warmly of her son, and it seems now as though Marnie will really __not__ go through with the planned robbery.

21) __MOTHER #2__ - at Marnie's childhood home.

Almost as now written, with talk of father and what happened to him, establishing black box under bed, and with much talk of marriage, slanted to lead us into thinking Marnie is seriously considering Mark now.

22) __THE RUTLAND ROBBERY__

23) REPRISE MONTAGE - rinsing out hair, station wagon, big head of Marnie riding, then into long shots, and down to camera and MARK!

18-22 SUSTAINED SCENES

**18** **Alfred Hitchcock** (British, 1899–1980) and
**Evan Hunter** (American, 1926–2005)
Excerpt from typed plot outline for *Marnie*, 1964
Alfred Hitchcock Papers, Margaret Herrick Library,
Academy of Motion Picture Arts and Sciences.
Courtesy of Universal Studios Licensing LLLP.

**19** **Alfred Hitchcock** (British, 1899–1980)
Sketch for *Marnie*, 1964
Ink on paper
14 x 8-1/2 inches
Alfred Hitchcock Papers, Margaret Herrick Library,
Academy of Motion Picture Arts and Sciences.
Courtesy of Universal Studios Licensing LLLP.

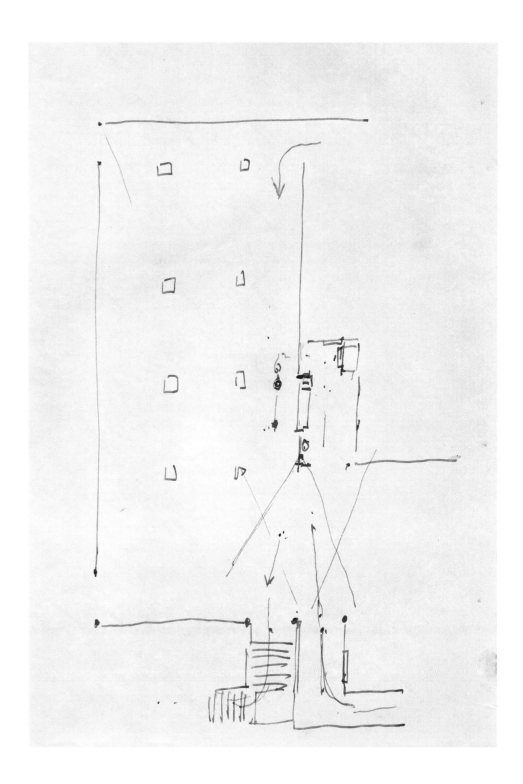

142     NEW SHOT - ARMSTRONG

A CLOSE VIEW of Armstrong's feet as they come level
with a corridor near the top of the staircase.  A
woman's foot suddenly sticks out from the corridor
entrance.  Armstrong is flung, face downward, falling
down the staircase.  As he falls, we see that he is
slightly behind and to the left of the main group
which is already filing down the staircase.  He falls,
hurtling past them.  The CAMERA RETREATS HOLDING HIM
IN CLOSE.  In the background, bewildered, the rest of
the group hurry down the stairs towards him.  He
lands with a crash at the foot of the staircase.  The
group clusters around him and we see that Armstrong
is not unconcious, but dazed by the fall.

                    VOICES OF GROUP
          Was is das?--what happened?
          Are you hurt?  Mein Gott!
          Professor?-- Michael?

                    A WOMAN'S VOICE
          We must get him to the clinic
          at once.  Gently, please.


143     INT. - CLINIC - DAY

A large closed eye fills the screen.  A thumb opens
the lid.  The eyelid flutters for a moment, then
stays open.  A tiny pinpoint of light searches the
iris of the eye.  The eyelid flutters again, and we
hear Armstrong's voice:

                    ARMSTRONG'S VOICE
                    (groans)
          What happened --how did I fall?

We now see the top half of a Woman's face. She holds
an opthalmoscope in front of her eye.

                    WOMAN DOCTOR
          You didn't fall.  I tripped you.
          Sorry, I overdid it, a bit.
          But I had to get you alone.


144     CLOSEUP - ARMSTRONG

looks at her astonished.


145     CLOSEUP - WOMAN DOCTOR

                                        (Continued)

20 **Brian Moore**  (British, 1921–1999)
Excerpt from typed script for *Torn Curtain*, 1966
Alfred Hitchcock Papers, Margaret Herrick Library,
Academy of Motion Picture Arts and Sciences.
Courtesy of Universal Studios Licensing LLLP.

21 **Alfred Hitchcock**  (British, 1899–1980)
Sketches for *Torn Curtain*, 1966
Graphite on paper
8 x 5 inches
Alfred Hitchcock Papers, Margaret Herrick Library,
Academy of Motion Picture Arts and Sciences.
Courtesy of Universal Studios Licensing LLLP.

The fall on the staircase

The art department often experimented with styles—in this case, the influence of drawings from the Works Progress Administration is visible—which meant it did not always strike the right tone or create images that would be replicated in the movie. Plate 22, a production design drawing from *Shadow of a Doubt*, shows the main set of characters, the Newton family, at the Santa Rosa train station. The sketch places the family in the background while still pulling the viewer's eye toward them and possesses a robust, muscular style. Neither the composition nor the style was reproduced in the movie.

Plates 23 and 24, also production design drawings from *Shadow of a Doubt*, are superb examples of how early drawings could establish the ultimate look, feel, and themes of a movie, in addition to mapping out a particular scene's set design. The sketches create a visual rhyme—images with similar content and mise-en-scène. In this instance both images depict a character reposing on a bed, facing to the right. The script reinforces the rhyme: she is named Charlie and he is her Uncle Charlie. When they are juxtaposed, the uncle's sinister and brooding daydreams menace Charlie's brighter and quieter imaginings. Together they convey the essence of *Shadow of a Doubt*.

22  **Harland Frazer** (American, 1895–1981)
Production design for *Shadow of a Doubt*, 1943
Photographic reproduction of graphite on paper
8 x 10 inches
Robert Boyle Papers, Margaret Herrick Library,
Academy of Motion Picture Arts and Sciences.
Courtesy of Universal Studios Licensing LLLP.

23  **Robert Boyle**  (American, born 1909)
Production design for *Shadow of a Doubt*, 1943
Photographic reproduction of graphite on paper
8 x 10 inches
Robert Boyle Papers, Margaret Herrick Library,
Academy of Motion Picture Arts and Sciences.
Courtesy of Universal Studios Licensing LLLP.

**24** **Dorothea Holt** (American, born 1910)
Production design for *Shadow of a Doubt*, 1943
Photographic reproduction of graphite on paper
8 x 10 inches
Robert Boyle Papers, Margaret Herrick Library,
Academy of Motion Picture Arts and Sciences.
Courtesy of Universal Studios Licensing LLLP.

Although sequential, plates 25–30 are not storyboards but production design drawings for *Shadow of a Doubt*. Their achievement is tonal, not technical. Unlike storyboards, they do not contain written blocking or camera instructions, shot numbers, or script excerpts. When compared with the film, each setting is different, and the angles from which images are drawn are much too high. These drawings capture the suspense of a climactic sequence. They portray Charlie after she first suspects her uncle of being a murderer—she's walking to the library to research the case.

In these drawings, the sleepy town of Santa Rosa has become a deeply foreboding place. The shadows of the trees suddenly seem dangerous; the wind blows ominously down the street. Only the library, which has just closed, looks safe. These drawings breathe high drama into otherwise banal action.

Thornton Wilder, along with Hitchcock, had created the characters and the drama of this moment, but production design artist Dorothea Holt gave it a visual dimension, transforming Santa Rosa into a threatening locale. Although the sequence was ultimately designed and shot differently, her visualization of it was essential to the evolution of *Shadow of a Doubt*.

25  **Dorothea Holt**  (American, born 1910)
Production design for *Shadow of a Doubt*, 1943
Photographic reproduction of graphite on paper
8 x 10 inches
Robert Boyle Papers, Margaret Herrick Library, Academy
of Motion Picture Arts and Sciences. Courtesy of
Universal Studios Licensing LLLP.

**26** **Dorothea Holt** (American, born 1910)
Production design for *Shadow of a Doubt*, 1943
Photographic reproduction of graphite on paper
8 x 10 inches
Robert Boyle Papers, Margaret Herrick Library,
Academy of Motion Picture Arts and Sciences.
Courtesy of Universal Studios Licensing LLLP.

**27** **Dorothea Holt** (American, born 1910)
Production design for *Shadow of a Doubt*, 1943
Photographic reproduction of graphite on paper
8 x 10 inches
Robert Boyle Papers, Margaret Herrick Library,
Academy of Motion Picture Arts and Sciences.
Courtesy of Universal Studios Licensing LLLP.

**28** **Dorothea Holt** (American, born 1910)
Production design for *Shadow of a Doubt*, 1943
Photographic reproduction of graphite on paper
8 x 10 inches
Robert Boyle Papers, Margaret Herrick Library,
Academy of Motion Picture Arts and Sciences.
Courtesy of Universal Studios Licensing LLLP.

**29** **Dorothea Holt** (American, born 1910)
Production design for *Shadow of a Doubt*, 1943
Photographic reproduction of graphite on paper
8 x 10 inches
Robert Boyle Papers, Margaret Herrick Library,
Academy of Motion Picture Arts and Sciences.
Courtesy of Universal Studios Licensing LLLP.

**30** **Dorothea Holt** (American, born 1910)
Production design for *Shadow of a Doubt*, 1943
Photographic reproduction of graphite on paper
8 x 10 inches
Robert Boyle Papers, Margaret Herrick Library,
Academy of Motion Picture Arts and Sciences.
Courtesy of Universal Studios Licensing LLLP.

Plate 31 shows a page from Hitchcock's shot list for the crow sequence in *The Birds*. A shot list records each shot in a given sequence. Plate 32 reproduces a storyboard based on this list and drawn by the art department.

Hitchcock goes into exacting detail about the types of shots and camera movements—pans, full shots, sweeps—as well as the number of birds and the distance of the camera from the action. The shot list outlines Hitchcock's techniques for building suspense—having the crows rise from behind the schoolhouse, for example, places them in the shot suddenly, without any camera movements. However, the list is not exhaustive: though it mentions a "pattering" of feet, it disregards other details of the sound design.

The shot list also highlights the contributions of production designer Robert Boyle, who worked alone for three months (before even Hitchcock was on the studio payroll) on the technical challenges of *The Birds*. During that time Boyle wrote an extensive report on a variety of techniques that would create the effect of attacking birds. The methods Hitchcock mentions in the shot list, such as "mechanical birds," came out of his discussions with Boyle.

④

27-28 A full screen of crows — about 50 or more. — the shoot off — the feet pattering. Suddenly the crows rise — the camera pans up with them.

28-29 The full shot showing the children running toward the camera - Annie herding them at the rear. The crows — about 200 - massing over the schoolhouse roof and descending toward the and reaching the running children. Shot as a plate with 6 or 7 children in front on a treadmill with the mechanical birds coming into top of screen as though continuing on from the plate. The birds swing around and among the foreground children. 15 feet

29-30 A side view of running children with Melanie in front urging them forward Birds fly between them 2 or 3 others wheel around 1 large one sweeps by in f.g. 4 feet.

**31 Alfred Hitchcock** (British, 1899–1980)
Handwritten shot list for *The Birds*, 1963
Alfred Hitchcock Papers, Margaret Herrick Library,
Academy of Motion Picture Arts and Sciences.
Courtesy of Universal Studios Licensing LLLP.

**32 Harold Michelson** (American, 1920–2007)
Storyboard for *The Birds*, 1963
Photostat of graphite on paper
11 x 8-1/2 inches
Alfred Hitchcock Papers, Margaret Herrick Library,
Academy of Motion Picture Arts and Sciences.
Courtesy of Universal Studios Licensing LLLP.

*Topaz* and *Family Plot* are the only two Hitchcock films for which extensive storyboards that cover many sequences in the movies are known to exist. They are the most explicit of any he created. They include not just renderings of each shot but detailed instructions for the camera operator, such as "start close on screen filling shot." By the time the first of these films went into preproduction, Hitchcock's longtime cinematographer, Robert Burks, and editor, George Tomasini, had both passed away. Hitchcock may have prepared more extensive storyboards, which specifically addressed the movie's cinematography and editing, because he did not have the security of working with key collaborators whose work he knew well.

Nevertheless, Hitchcock continued to refine the project, departing from the storyboard in small but often significant ways. For example, in shot 98 (plate 33) the camera "eases back" to the left, not the right, and shot 113 (plate 35) is not from the point of view [P.O.V.] of George Lumley (Bruce Dern). Instead, the sequence includes a tracking shot of the gas station attendant approaching Lumley's car. The *Topaz* storyboards include the original ending (plate 41), an old-fashioned duel, which although filmed did not appear in the final cut of the movie.

**33** **Thomas Wright** (biography unknown)
Storyboard for *Family Plot*, 1975
Photostat of graphite on paper
11 x 8-1/2 inches
Alfred Hitchcock Papers, Margaret Herrick Library,
Academy of Motion Picture Arts and Sciences.
Courtesy of Universal Studios Licensing LLLP.

**34** **Thomas Wright** (biography unknown)
Storyboard for *Family Plot*, 1975
Photostat of graphite on paper
8-1/2 x 11 inches
Alfred Hitchcock Papers, Margaret Herrick Library,
Academy of Motion Picture Arts and Sciences.
Courtesy of Universal Studios  Licensing LLLP.

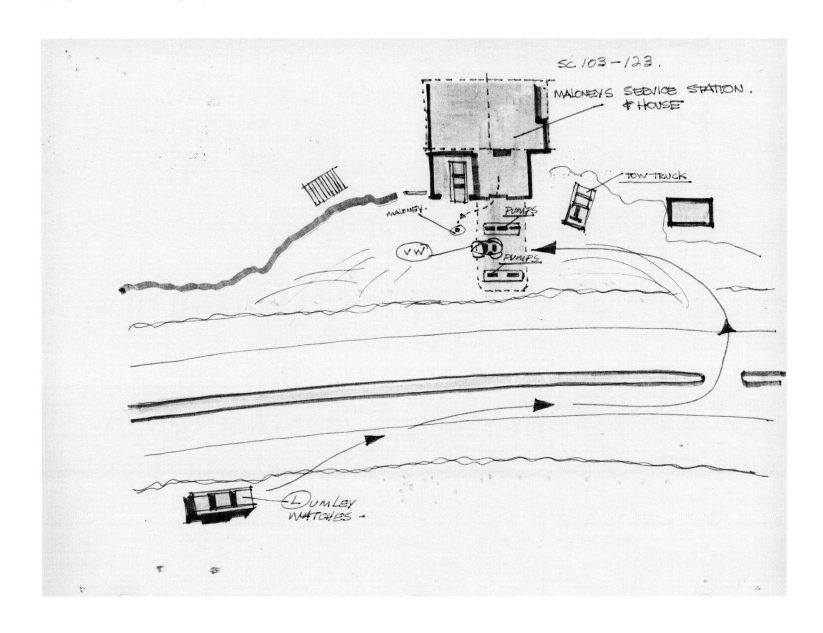

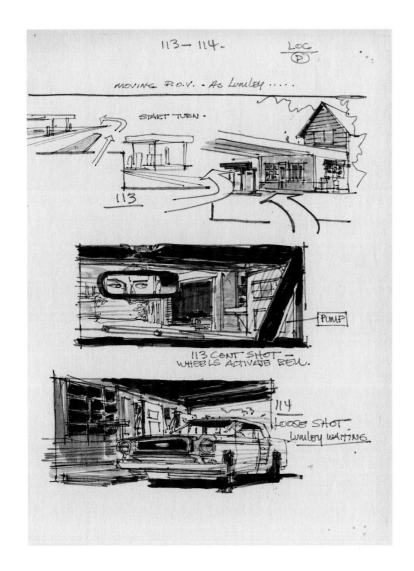

113 - 114 -                    LOC
                                (P)

MOVING P.O.V. - AS LUMLEY .....

START TURN -

113

113 CONT SHOT -
WHEELS ACTIVATE BELL.

PUMP

114
LOOSE SHOT
LUMLEY WAITING

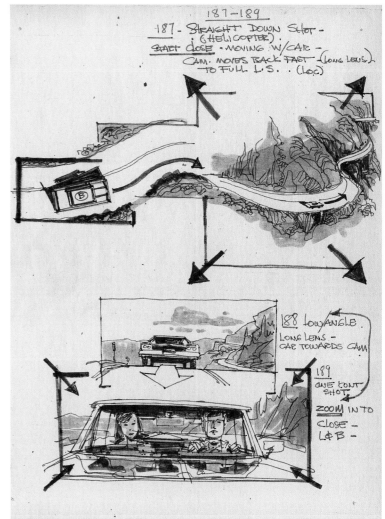

187 - 189

187 - STRAIGHT DOWN SHOT -
(HELICOPTER).
START CLOSE - MOVING W/CAR -
CAM. MOVES BACK FAST (LONG LENS)
TO FULL L.S. . (LOC)

188 LOW ANGLE -
LONG LENS -
CAR TOWARDS CAM

189
ONE CONT
SHOT -

ZOOM INTO

CLOSE -
L & B -

35  **Thomas Wright** (biography unknown)
    Storyboard for *Family Plot*, 1975
    Photostat of graphite on paper
    11 x 8-1/2 inches
    Alfred Hitchcock Papers,
    Margaret Herrick Library, Academy
    of Motion Picture Arts and Sciences.
    Courtesy of Universal Studios
    Licensing LLLP.

36  **Thomas Wright** (biography unknown)
    Storyboard for *Family Plot*, 1975
    Photostat of graphite on paper
    11 x 8-1/2 inches
    Alfred Hitchcock Papers,
    Margaret Herrick Library, Academy
    of Motion Picture Arts and Sciences.
    Courtesy of Universal Studios
    Licensing LLLP.

37  **Thomas Wright** (biography unknown)
    Storyboard for *Family Plot*, 1975
    Photostat of graphite on paper
    11 x 8-1/2 inches
    Alfred Hitchcock Papers,
    Margaret Herrick Library, Academy
    of Motion Picture Arts and Sciences.
    Courtesy of Universal Studios
    Licensing LLLP.

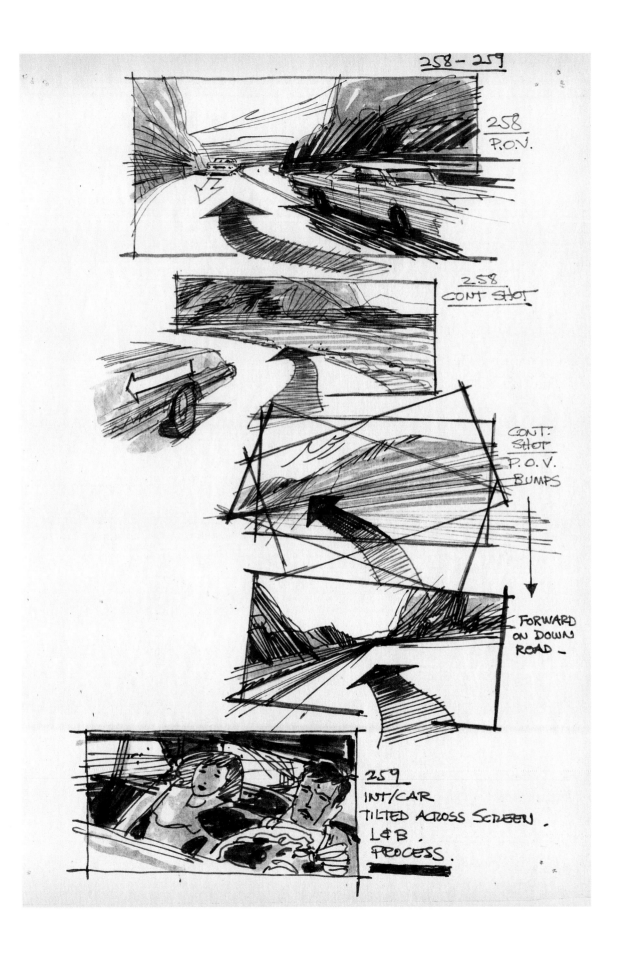

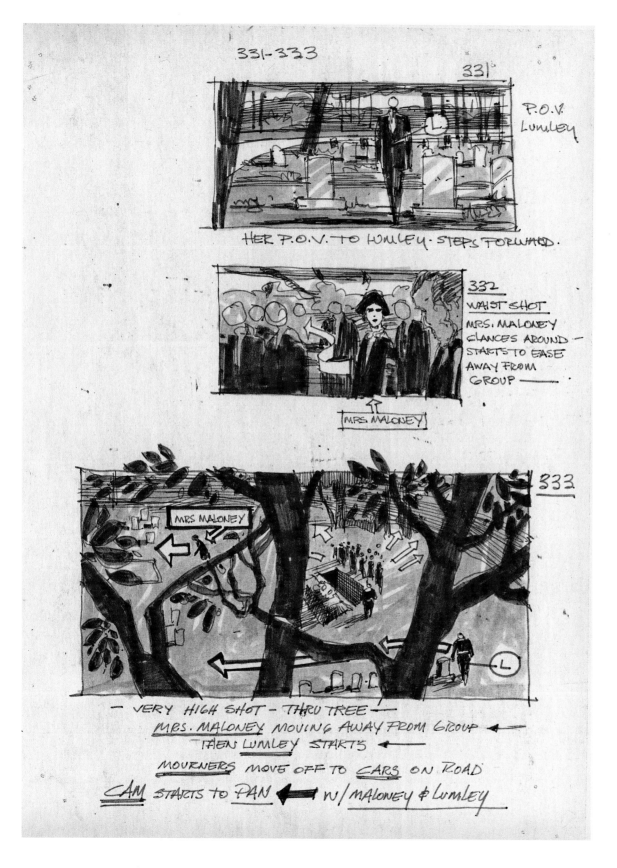

331-333

331

P.O.V.
Lumley

HER P.O.V. TO LUMLEY. STEPS FORWARD.

332
WAIST SHOT
MRS. MALONEY
GLANCES AROUND -
STARTS TO EASE
AWAY FROM
GROUP —

MRS MALONEY

333

MRS MALONEY

L

— VERY HIGH SHOT - THRU TREE —
MRS. MALONEY MOVING AWAY FROM GROUP ◄
THEN LUMLEY STARTS ◄
MOURNERS MOVE OFF TO CARS ON ROAD
CAM STARTS TO PAN ◄ W/ MALONEY & LUMLEY

38  **Thomas Wright** (biography unknown)
Storyboard for *Family Plot*, 1975
Photostat of graphite on paper
11 x 8-1/2 inches
Alfred Hitchcock Papers, Margaret Herrick
Library, Academy of Motion Picture Arts
and Sciences. Courtesy of Universal Studios
Licensing LLLP.

39  **Thomas Wright** (biography unknown)
Storyboard for *Topaz*, 1969
Photostat of graphite on paper
8-1/2 x 11 inches
Alfred Hitchcock Papers, Margaret Herrick
Library, Academy of Motion Picture Arts
and Sciences. Courtesy of Universal Studios
Licensing LLLP.

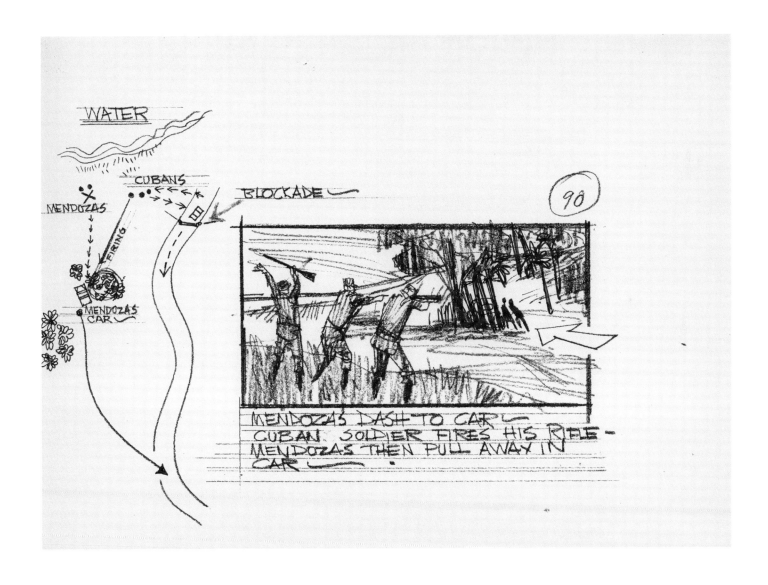

WATER

CUBANS

MENDOZAS

FIRING

BLOCKADE

MENDOZAS
CAR

90

MENDOZAS DASH TO CAR
CUBAN SOLDIER FIRES HIS RIFLE -
MENDOZAS THEN PULL AWAY IN
CAR

ZOOM IN ON
NEWSPAPER →

**40 Thomas Wright** (biography unknown)
Storyboard for *Topaz*, 1969
Photostat of graphite on paper
9 x 12 inches
Alfred Hitchcock Papers, Margaret Herrick
Library, Academy of Motion Picture Arts
and Sciences. Courtesy of Universal Studios
Licensing LLLP.

**41 Thomas Wright** (biography unknown)
Storyboard for *Topaz*, 1969
Photostat of graphite on paper
11 x 8-1/2 inches
Alfred Hitchcock Papers, Margaret Herrick
Library, Academy of Motion Picture Arts
and Sciences. Courtesy of Universal Studios
Licensing LLLP.

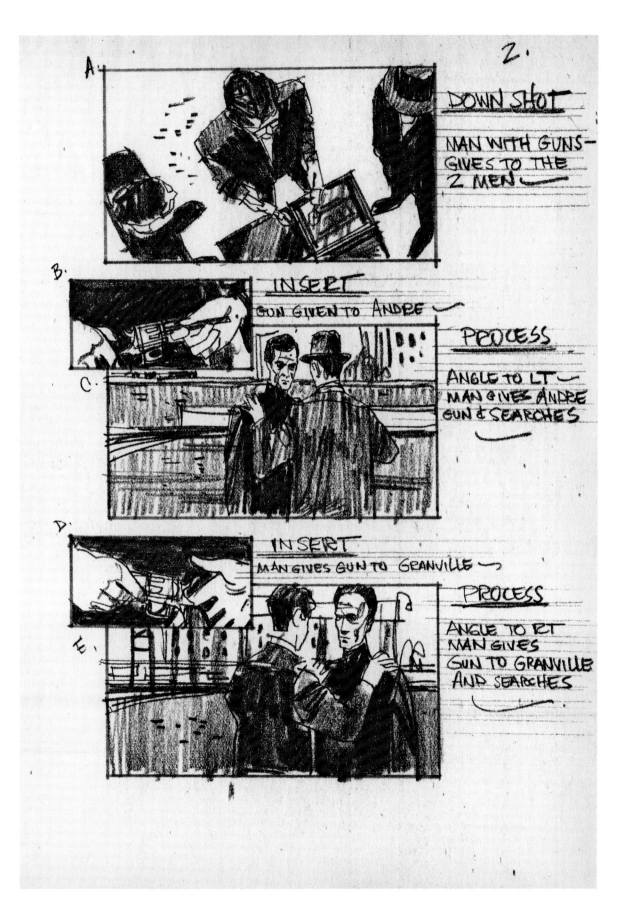

Plates 42 and 43 are storyboards from *Vertigo* that were drawn to guide the second unit, a small crew that films scenes that do not include the principal actors or sets. In *Vertigo* the second unit was sent to San Francisco to shoot footage of the city.

Scenes 185B and 185D in plate 42 were shot on location with doubles. In this case, doubles are actors who are indistinguishable from the leads at a distance. The second unit also shot the San Francisco Bay as the backdrop to scenes that James Stewart and Kim Novak would act out in the studio, such as scenes 185E and 185G in plate 43. Such precise instructions and story-boards for the second unit were important as they often worked independently while Hitch-cock was on set with the first unit.

Sc. 185A Scottie sits in car watching her.
She does not move. Transp. plus car.

Sc. 185B Madeleine slowly starts to walk
toward the sea. Location with double.

Sc. 185C Scottie opens car door and jumps out.
Transp. plus car.

Sc. 185D Madeleine has stopped and turned.
Scottie joins her. Location with doubles.

42 Unknown illustrator and **Henry Bumstead**
(American, 1915–2006), production designer
Storyboard for *Vertigo*, 1958
Photostat of graphite on paper
8-1/2 x 11 inches
Alfred Hitchcock Papers, Margaret Herrick Library,
Academy of Motion Picture Arts and Sciences.
Courtesy of Universal Studios Licensing LLLP.

43 Unknown illustrator and **Henry Bumstead**
(American, 1915–2006), production designer
Storyboard for *Vertigo*, 1958
Photostat of graphite on paper
8-1/2 x 11 inches
Alfred Hitchcock Papers, Margaret Herrick Library,
Academy of Motion Picture Arts and Sciences.
Courtesy of Universal Studios Licensing LLLP.

Sc. 185E Madeleine and Scottie play scene
at cypress tree. Transp. plus studio set.
Madeleine turns and exits scene.

Sc. 185F Madeleine running toward the edge
of the land. Scottie following.
Location with doubles.

Sc. 185G Scottie catches her and holds her.
Location with doubles.

Sc. 185H Madeleine and Scottie play scene
The wind blows and the waves dash up
against the rocks throwing up a curtain
of spray. Transp.

Plates 44–50 from *Saboteur* blur the line between production design drawings and storyboards. In 1941 prior to filming, producer David O. Selznick had Hitchcock under contract and was eager to sell the *Saboteur* project to a studio for immediate production. The project was rushed. They did not have time to storyboard.

This 4x4 grid of rough sketches (plate 44) stood in for a storyboard of the Statue of Liberty sequence. Specific grids were developed into production design sketches, some of which would appear nearly unchanged in the film (plates 46, 47, and 49). Others, like the sketch of the two men grappling by the torch (plate 45), would be significantly altered during the production.

These sketches did not establish the order of the shots, a step that organizes shooting, ensures narrative continuity, and is a key function of storyboards. Because of the rushed production schedule, Hitchcock sketched crude storyboards for certain action-filled sequences. Included here are shots 20–22 of the Statue of Liberty sequence (plate 50) from his quickly drawn storyboards.

44 **John De Cuir** (American, 1918–1991)
Production design for *Saboteur*, 1942
Photographic reproduction of graphite on paper
8 x 10 inches
Robert Buyle Papers, Margaret Herrick Library,
Academy of Motion Picture Arts and Sciences.
Courtesy of Universal Studios Licensing LLLP.

131

45 **John De Cuir**  (American, 1918–1991)
Production design for *Saboteur*, 1942
Photographic reproduction of graphite on paper
8 x 10 inches
Robert Boyle Papers, Margaret Herrick Library,
Academy of Motion Picture Arts and Sciences.
Courtesy of Universal Studios Licensing LLLP.

46 **John De Cuir**  (American, 1918–1991)
Production design for *Saboteur*, 1942
Photographic reproduction of graphite on paper
8 x 10 inches
Robert Boyle Papers, Margaret Herrick Library,
Academy of Motion Picture Arts and Sciences.
Courtesy of Universal Studios Licensing LLLP.

133

**47** **John De Cuir** (American, 1918–1991)
Production design for *Saboteur*, 1942
Photographic reproduction of graphite on paper
8 x 10 inches
Robert Boyle Papers, Margaret Herrick
Library, Academy of Motion Picture Arts and
Sciences. Courtesy of Universal Studios
Licensing LLLP.

**48** **John De Cuir** (American, 1918–1991)
Production design for *Saboteur*, 1942
Photographic reproduction of graphite on paper
8 x 10 inches
Robert Boyle Papers, Margaret Herrick
Library, Academy of Motion Picture Arts and
Sciences. Courtesy of Universal Studios
Licensing LLLP.

**49  John De Cuir** (American, 1918–1991)
Production design for *Saboteur*, 1942
Photographic reproduction of graphite on paper
8 x 10 inches
Robert Boyle Papers, Margaret Herrick Library,
Academy of Motion Picture Arts and Sciences.
Courtesy of Universal Studios Licensing LLLP.

**50  Alfred Hitchcock** (British, 1899–1980)
Storyboard for *Saboteur*, 1942
Graphite on paper
11 x 8-1/2 inches
Robert Boyle Papers, Margaret Herrick Library,
Academy of Motion Picture Arts and Sciences.
Courtesy of Universal Studios Licensing LLLP.

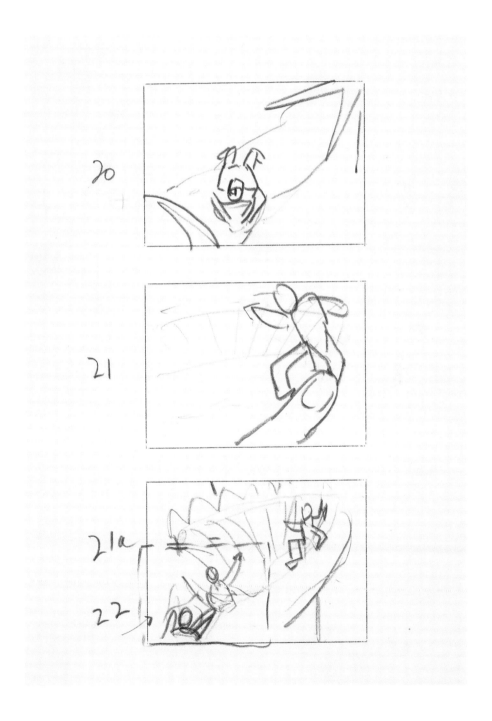

Separate camera angle drawings were usually
made for difficult scenes in Hitchcock's films.
Plates 50 and 51 are from *North by Northwest*.
They depict the camera placements and angles for
the scene in which Roger Thornhill (Cary Grant) is
kidnapped from the Plaza Hotel. The sketches,
although not drawn to scale, carefully establish
the space, showing the same doorways and
seating arrangements that are in the final film.
Characters are designated by letters: *T* stands for
Thornhill and *BB* for the bellboy. The four camera
angles labeled 16, 16A, 16b, and 16d establish
Thornhill's entrance to the bar. Camera angle 18
is a shot from the kidnappers' point of view.

Plate 52, the third drawing in this sequence,
is from *Saboteur* and depicts the scene in which
Frank Fry (Norman Lloyd) is pursued by the police
into Radio City Music Hall. The drawing establish-
es the blocking for the police (the encircled *P*)
and for Fry, who jumps onto the stage. It also
shows the camera angles for two crowd shots.
Plate 53, the fourth drawing, is a camera angle
drawing from *Lifeboat,* which is much more com-
pact because the action is entirely on a lifeboat.

**51**  Unknown illustrator and **Robert Burks**
(American, 1910–1968), cinematographer
Camera angle diagram for *North by Northwest*, 1958
Graphite on paper
11 x 8-1/2 inches
Alfred Hitchcock Papers, Margaret Herrick Library,
Academy of Motion Picture Arts and Sciences.
NORTH BY NORTHWEST © Turner Entertainment Co.
A Warner Bros. Entertainment Company.
All Rights Reserved.

**52**  Unknown illustrator and **Robert Burks**
(American, 1910–1968), cinematographer
Camera angle diagram for *North by Northwest*, 1958
Graphite on paper
11 x 8-1/2 inches
Alfred Hitchcock Papers, Margaret Herrick Library,
Academy of Motion Picture Arts and Sciences.
NORTH BY NORTHWEST © Turner Entertainment Co.
A Warner Bros. Entertainment Company.
All Rights Reserved.

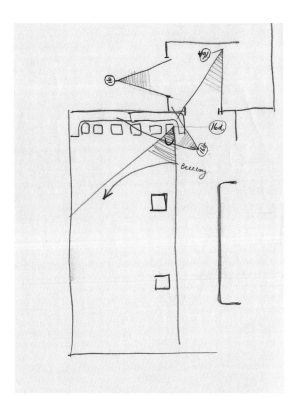

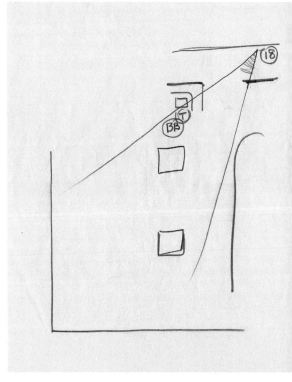

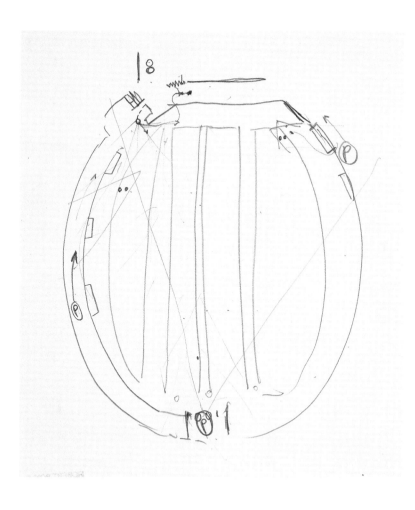

53  **Alfred Hitchcock** (British, 1899–1980), illustrator and
**Joseph Valentine** (American, 1900–1949), cinematographer
Camera angle diagram for *Saboteur*, 1942
Graphite on paper
9-1/2 x 8 inches
Robert Boyle Papers, Margaret Herrick Library, Academy
of Motion Picture Arts and Sciences.
Courtesy of Universal Studios Licensing LLLP.

54  Unknown illustrator and **Glen MacWilliams**
(American, 1898–1984), cinematographer
Camera angle diagram for *Lifeboat*, 1943
Photostat with pen and color pencil additions
11 x 8-1/2 inches
Alfred Hitchcock Papers, Margaret Herrick Library,
Academy of Motion Picture Arts and Sciences.

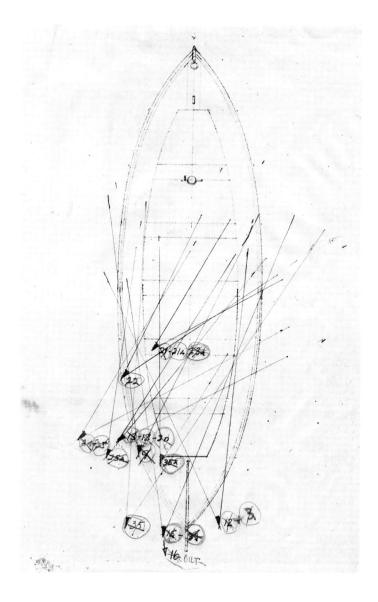

The camera angle diagram in plate 55 is remarkably dense. It is for the crop-dusting sequence in *North by Northwest*, suggested by the multiple representations of a plane, the crossroads underneath the web of camera angles, and the encircled *T* for the character of Roger Thornhill (Cary Grant). The shot numbers correspond directly to the numbers on the *Continuity for Crop-Dusting Sequence, Scene 115, October 6* (plates 56a–d).

The shots that are boxed together indicate that they were to be shot from the same camera setup and angle. The letter *P* following a shot number refers to "process shot," meaning two or more images will be combined into one. In this case footage of the plane would be combined in the studio with footage of Thornhill running. The dotted lines linking encircled letters *T* in shots 36, 42, and 43 refer to Thornhill's running away from the plane, and the blocking would be accompanied by tracking movement from the camera.

Robert Boyle, production designer for *North by Northwest*, has said that the production timeline moved so quickly that there was not enough time to storyboard the crop-dusting sequence. However, since these documents are so detailed, and Hitchcock's department heads had been visualizing the movie with him since preproduction, the continuity memo and diagrams were enough for filming.

55  Unknown illustrator and **Robert Burks**
(American, 1919–1968), cinematographer
Camera angle diagram for *North by Northwest*, 1958
Graphite on paper
8-1/2 x 11
Alfred Hitchcock Papers, Margaret Herrick
Library, Academy of Motion Picture Arts and  Sciences.
NORTH BY NORTHWEST © Turner Entertainment Co.
A Warner Bros. Entertainment Company. All Rights
Reserved.

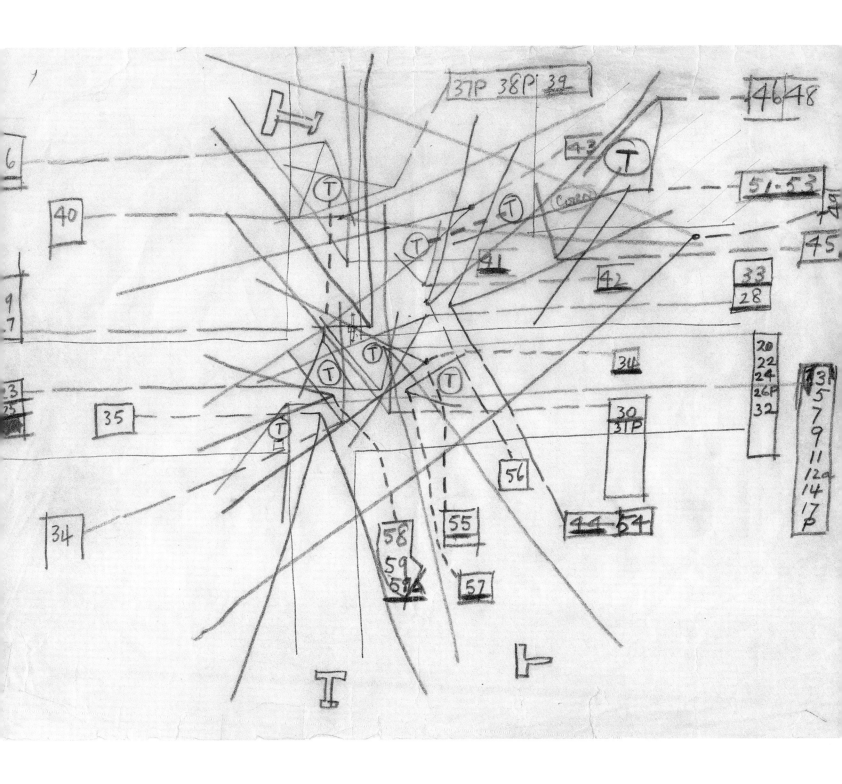

CONTINUITY FOR CROP DUSTING SEQUENCE, SCENE 115, OCTOBER 6

1. High Shot - Bus arriving - Man out.

2. Lonely figure (Sketch 3)
   (Shot Monday, Slate 211)

3. Waist Shot - Thornhill looks about him in four directions.
3A a. Process plate for all Thornhill's Close Ups.

4. a. P.O.V.
      Through wide fence onto plowed field.
      (Shot Monday, Slate 203X)
   b. P.O.V.
      Empty road from where bus came
      (Shot Monday, Slate 201)
   c. P.O.V.
      Sae West Brush
      (Shot Monday, Slate 202X)
   d. P.O.V.
      Corn Field
      (Shot Monday, Slate 204X)
   e. P.O.V.
      Empty road ahead
      (Shot Monday, Slate 210X)

5. Closer Shot - Thornhill glances at ~~west with satisfaction~~ wristwatch and then
   looks up road expectantly.

6. Car (Mercury) coming down road left to right. Whips by. Whip Shot
   (Shot Monday, Slate 208)

7. Semi Close Up. Thornhill's head whips around. He turns back and looks
   up road.- Nothing. His expression changes as he hears a car and turns
   back in the direction of the previous car.

8. Second Whip Shot - Limousine coming along at not too fast a pace.
   Again ~~car~~ slow whips by.
   (Shot Monday, Slate 209X)

9. Semi Close Up - Thornhill's head turns with changing expression from
   slight apprehension to normal expectancy.

10. P.O.V. As the limousine is well down the road a truck comes.  It approache
    at fast speed and whips by right to left.

11. Wind of rushing truck causes Thornhill to step back a shade.  Overlop
    truck whizzing by.  Shoot ~~all~~ alternates with and without dust.  He

12. Full figure of Thornhill standing lonely once more.  There is a chugging
    sound off - he takes a step forward.
    (Shot Monday, Slate 216)

A a.  Closer shot of Thornhill as in #12.

13. P.O.V. Green sedan is turning around from corn field.
    (Shot Monday, Slate 213)

14. Waist Shot - Thornhill as he watches green sedan and reacts to action in
    #15. *(Thom hands woman pocket, walks forward & takes hands out)*

15. P.O.V. Sedan comes to stop, man gets out. Wife inside, turns car. Man is
    left standing alone as sedan goes away.

    INTERCUT THIS WITH THORNHILL WATCHING ALL THIS.
    (Shot Monday, Slate 213)

16. Semi Long Shot two men isolated. One, one side of the road opposite the
    other. *Farmer hands behind back.*
    (Shot Monday, Slate 212)

17. Semi Close Up - Thornhill looking across at man. He dusts himself off. *open jacket - lips*

18. Semi Long Shot - The man from Thornhill's P.O.V. He looks back to Thornhill.
    (Shot Monday, Slate 213)

19. Medium Shot - Thornhill come to decision. He crosses the road diagonally.
    Camera panning with him until the man comes into picture right of screen--
    set for dialogue scene. *dolly shot 19B*
    *19B alternate to dolly shot 19B*

19 A a. Bus approaching to intercut dialogue scene #19.
    (Shot on Monday, Slate 215)

20. P.O.V. of Airplane.

21. Back to shot of two men (Waist). Bus pulls up to stop. Farmer gets on
    bus which pulls away. Thornhill left looking off at crop duster plane. *jacket open - hands hips*

22. The crop duster is making a turn on left-hand side of screen. *P.O.V. Thornhill*

23. Waist shot - Thornhill watching it. *jacket open - lips*

24. Plane coming nearer, and nearer, and nearer to camera. *Same P.O.V.*

25. Reverse - Thornhill viewing with alarm. *He drops out of picture.*

26. Objective Shot - STUDIO Plane diving down on Thornhill, who ducks to ground. *drops in later on*

    NOTE: Plane REQUIRED FOR THIS SHOT, LOOKS OFF

27. Plane raising away from its dive and going away from us. *same P.O.V. for ground*

28. Full Figure - Thornhill rises to his feet--looks after the plane and
    looks about him desperately wondering where he can go. He is suddenly
    rooted as he sees. _____ + alternate - Bob's shot Reverse on Thornhill Pan
    *The Plane*                                        *all action in 28 & 30*

29. P.O.V. Now coming towards him in line with the farmer's road. *into ditch from*
    *Farmer's rd - shot, back to*

30. Medium Shot - Thornhill, thoroughly alarmed dives off into ditch, camera
    panning him. He crouches down as plane is making a dive.
    *30A Bob's alternate*

31. STUDIO SHOT - Plane makes a dive over Close Up Thornhill in ditch. *PLATE*
    Wheels go through top of picture, Thornhill watching.
    *Plate 251 Action     Give as plus as 30     (Match ditch in studio)*

143

32. P.O.V. Plane going away again.

33. Medium Shot - Thornhill gets out of ditch and runs toward an approaching
    car. He tries to stop (by Robertson sign) but car goes on.

34. Close Shot - Thornhill looking after departing car. He looks off and
    sees _____.

35. P.O.V. Plane turning and coming down above road opposite farmer's road.

36. Waist shot - Shooting over Thornhill's shoulder - plane is approaching
    him. Thournhill turns and runs toward camera. Camera tracks back. We
    now have a picture of Thornhill running with occasional frantick glances
    over his shoulder as the plane approaches him. The plane gains on Thorn-
    hill and dives close to him as he drops to ground out of picture.

37. STUDIO SHOT - Thornhill drops onto side road as the wheels again go
    above him. Bullets hit the road between Thornhill and camera.
    (Process plate required)

38. Alternate - See sketch 39 for alternate shot taken on as Thornhill
    runs under passing wheel. ( Process plate required)

39. Close Shot - Thornhill rising in road. He looks off and sees STUDIO .

40. Long Shot - Corn as Sketch 41

41. Medium Shot - Shooting East Northeast. Thornhill, after looking at corn
    field, rises and dusts off. Plane to right in the background is beginning
    to make a right to left sweep in a forward turn. (Wing over)

42. Closer up, Waist hight - Starting with stationary camera. Dolly profile
    shot of Thornhill running with 2n3 glances over his shoulder left to
    right. After short run of camera, camera stops and Thornhill runs out
    of picture.

43. P.O.V. Dolly Shot - Camera moving backwards as though Thornhill, seeing
    plane beginning to make a turn to come towards Thornhill.
    (Shot with 50 m.m. and 35 m.m. lenses)

44. Thornhill dives from left of scene full figure and dives onto ground
    (Back field view)

45. Flash - Skimming shot of leaves moving as Thornhill dives into the corn
    and weaves short way through it. The shimmering stops and corn still.

46. Medium Shot - Thornhill lying doggo without any movement in the corn.

47. Objective Shot - Long shot the plane diving towards the corn and turning
    away.

48. Close Shot Thornhill- A dolly of set in his face but still lying doggo.

49. Long Shot - Corn tabbed in the corner of the picture. The plane turns
    and now comes toward camera again. This time it starts to exclude
    dust. It swerves toward camera excluding dust.

50. STUDIO SHOT (Sky backing) - Close shot Thornhill - Roar of plane overhead. Thornhill's expression changes as asphyxiating dust falls all around him. He begins to cough and sneeze,etc. Camera dollies into close up shot. He needs air. He rises out of corn, takes a deep breath and goes off.

51. Long Shot - From corn field view point. In far distance is double gasoline truck with corn in foreground. P.O.V.

52. Close up Thornhill dives out of picture, camera left (Studio Shot)

53. Double for Thornhill - Long Shot - Shooting towards the highway. The flying fall of Thornhill diving toward the highway and in the distance truck approaching.

54. Flash - Sky Shot - The plane circling after the corn dusting failure. This should be shot at a reasonable distance away.

55. Semi Long Shot - Thornhill diving onto the roadway, braces himself against the advancing truck which is only a short distance from him. He watches it frantically, at the same time looking desperately off screen to the right.

56. Flash - The plane coming down the highway after Thornhill.

57. Medium Shot - The frantically waving arms of Thornhill.

58. The truck advancing on him as it swerves with a screech of brakes.

59. Thornhill (Double) losing his nerve, tries to dive away and slips between the wheels of the truck.

60. Flash - Low Shot of the plane swooping down with the big wheel in the foreground, coming to a screech and the plane dives at the same moment.
    75 m.m. lenses

61. Miniature Impact

There are more than 40 extant shooting story-boards for *Lifeboat*, two of which are shown here (plates 57–58). The shooting storyboards were used during filming to plan shots. In effect they were the last documents made during prepro-duction.

These shooting storyboards also give evi-dence of revisions made during the production. For example, two lines of dialogue have been added (plate 61), and the original storyboard sketch on plate 60 has been modified with hand-written directions underneath—"Reverse with sail in B G [background] all looking left"—and resketched per those instructions at the bottom of the page. The artist of the storyboard is not identified, but the drawing at the bottom has the oval-shaped heads typical of Hitchcock's hand.

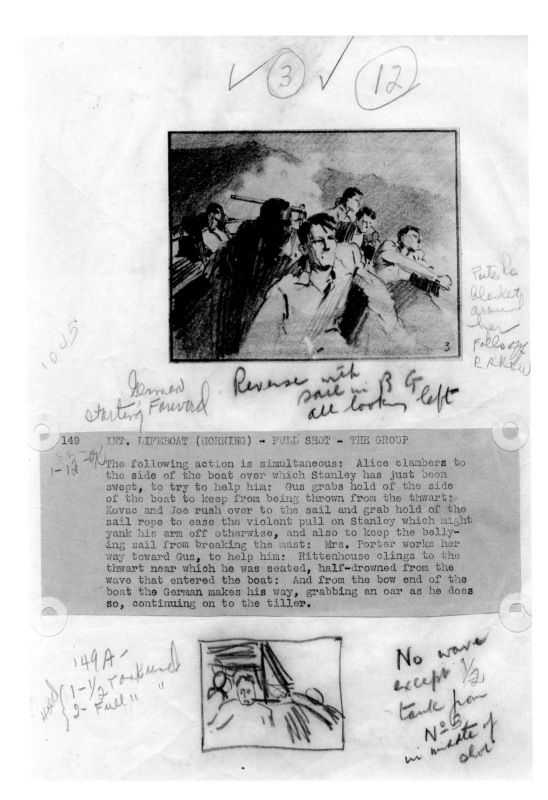

**57** Unknown illustrator and **Alfred Hitchcock**
(British, 1899–1980), director
Shooting storyboard for *Lifeboat*, 1943
Photostat of graphite on paper with typed paper
addition, revisions, notes, and sketch
11 x 8-1/2 inches
Alfred Hitchcock Papers, Margaret Herrick Library,
Academy of Motion Picture Arts and Sciences.
Lifeboat © 1944 Twentieth Century Fox.
All rights reserved.

**58** Unknown illustrator and **Alfred Hitchcock**
(British, 1899–1980), director
Shooting storyboard for *Lifeboat*, 1943
Photostat of graphite on paper with typed paper
addition and notes
11 x 8-1/2 inches
Alfred Hitchcock Papers, Margaret Herrick Library,
Academy of Motion Picture Arts and Sciences.
Lifeboat © 1944 Twentieth Century Fox.
All rights reserved.

147

In addition to his collaborations during production and preproduction, Hitchcock worked closely with numerous publicists throughout his career. His image and reputation were critical to the success of his films. With his publicists Hitchcock honed a widely recognized public persona, a process well documented in memos, such as plates 59 and 60, that also communicate the tension implicit in his public image. While his name and likeness were synonymous with suspense and mass entertainment, Hitchcock also promoted himself as an artist.

10M 12-44 L-C

VANGUARD FILMS, INC.
CULVER CITY, CALIFORNIA

Inter-Office Communication

TO     MR. HITCHCOCK          DATE August 24, 1945

FROM    PAUL MacNAMARA

SUBJECT   SPELLBOUND TRAILER

The trailer on "Spellbound," seems to me, could be much more ingenious.

I have talked to Selznick regarding the idea of making a new one and making it about you.

He agrees and thinks it would be a good idea.

Roughly, my idea was that you would discuss on the screen in lecture fashion the fact that everyone is a potential murderer, etc., etc.

There might be direct questions that you would ask the audience -- "do you know that the person next to you might be a potential murderer" -- "do you know that in your own mind you, too, might be a murderer," etc., etc.

Other emotions might be touched on in which audience participation would be included (including some laughs), "some of you are holding hands," etc., etc.

However, no clips of the picture would be used except in which your voice would be the sound and your explanation as to why it was handled that way would be that every bit of the picture "Spellbound" was so important to the plot that it was decided not to show to audiences anywhere any part of the picture in a piece-meal state. (The use of the clips in this fashion, however, would show the stars).

Perhaps the thing should be presented as a short rather than as a trailer.

Undoubtedly, Dr. Romm might be able to provide us with some questions that would be helpful in the preparation of a script.

In any case, I think that there is a basically good idea here and with the proper development we might be able to work out a sensational advance salesman for the picture "Spellbound."

What do you think?

                            PM

PM:eh

WILLIAM BLOWITZ - MAGDALENE MASKEL

6305 YUCCA STREET
HOLLYWOOD 28, CALIF.
HOllywood 2-3291

MEMO FROM: WILLIAM BLOWITZ                      Date: 3-19-62

TO:        ALFRED HITCHCOCK

SUBJECT:   THE BIRDS -- advertising, publicity,
                       merchandising --


Everything that is done in connection with THE BIRDS must
lead to the eventual merchandising of the finished film.
We are not talking about a nit-picking campaign, with
fragments of stories seeping out during production.  In
essence, what we are talking about is the PSYCHO campaign,
yet done in such a fashion that no one will say "They're
doing a good job of copying the PSYCHO campaign."  But,
rather, "Hitchcock is doing for THE BIRDS in merchandising
what he did with PSYCHO, but different."  If that appears
elliptical, we know of no other way to put it.  To re-create
the essence of a campaign without appearing to use the same
elements is a perfectly acceptable concept.  With that in
mind, let's take the various elements and examine them:

DATE OF RELEASE            The focal point of the campaign
                           will be the time of release.  All
magazine stories and layouts, special TV material, ads,
trailers and merchandising concept will be developed to hit
this point in time as simultaneously as possible.  We are
aware of the difficulty in pin-pointing this date this early,
but have discussed the necessity for a three-month period
in which to plan towards this definite date.

In this same area will come the knowledge on our part of the
distributor, so we can start to work with (or for) that
company.

ALFRED HITCHCOCK           The star of this picture, as with
                           PSYCHO, is Alfred Hitchcock.
Therefore, a pivotal element in publicity and advertising will
be Hitchcock.  In the notes on the magazine campaign, the
trailer and ads, all of this is emphasized.  The point of the
campaign is to sell tickets to THE BIRDS; Hitchcock will be
a principal element.

'TIPPI' HEDREN             As discussed several times, the
                           campaign on 'Tippi' is to be handled
in such a fashion that she becomes a desirable story, not one

# Index

Page numbers in *italics* refer to images

## A

*Alfred Hitchcock Hour*, 65, 73

*Alfred Hitchcock Presents*, 65–66, 73

"Alfred Hitchcock Resents" (Hitchcock), 72

Allardice, James, 63, 66, 69, 72, 73

American Film Institute, 75

Anderson, Judith, 32

Anthelme, Paul (pen name for Paul Bourde), 53, 56, 58–59, 60

Anthony, Bruno (character in *Strangers on a Train*), 38, 50, 61

*Anxiety of Influence, The* (Bloom), 55

Archibald, William, 61

architectural plans, 19–21

Armstrong, Michael (character in *Torn Curtain*), 104

"Arthur" (television show), 67

*Ashenden, the Secret Agent* (Maugham), 57

Astruc, Alexandre, 49

Auber, Brigitte, 52

Ault, Marie, 31

## B

Bagdasarian, Ross, 30

Balcon, Michael, 4, 54, 55

Balestrero, Manny (character in *The Wrong Man*), 38, 50, *50*

Balestrero, Rose (character in *The Wrong Man*), *50*

Barr, Alfred H., Jr., 4

Barry, Iris, 4

Bartók, Béla, 30

Basevi, James, *97*

Bates, Norman (character in *Psycho*), 44–46, 47

Baxter, Anne, 59

Bazin, André, 52, 79n5 (chap. 1)

Bel Geddes, Barbara, *35*, 35–36, *37*

Benson (character in *Suspicion*), 41

Benson, Sally, 102

Bergman, Ingrid, 49, 50, 58, 60

Bernstein, Leonard, 30

Bernstein, Sidney, *10*, 11, 53, 60

BIP (British International Pictures), 4, 55

*Birds, The* (1963): Boyle and, 13, 18, 22, 88, *89*, 118; characters in, 24; collaboration on, x–xi, 8, 9, 13; costumes for, *12*; drawings and storyboards, 18, 22, 24, *89*, *98*, *110*, *119*; set of, *5*; shot list for, *118*; typed memo for, *149*

*Birds, The* (du Maurier), xi, 13, 22, 88

*Blackmail* (1929), 38–40, 56, 57

Bloom, Harold, 55

Blowitz, William, *149*

Bordier (character in *Nos deux consciences*), 53

Borzage, Frank, 53

Bourde, Paul, 58–59, 60

Boyle, Robert: *The Birds* and, 13, 18, 22, 88, *89*, 118; Mount Rushmore house and, 19–20, 27, 100, *101*; *North by Northwest* and, 19–20, 27, 100, *101*, 140; production designs, *89*, *99*, *110*; roles of, xi, 21

British International Pictures (BIP), 4, 55

Brown, Kay, 102, *103*

*Bruges-la-Morte* (Rodenbach), 36

Buchan, John, 57

Bumstead, Henry, xi, *2*, 19–20, *128–129*

Burks, Robert, *6*, 21, *31*, 120, *138*, *141–145*

Burr, Raymond, 30

## C

"Cadaver, The" (television show), 67

*Cahiers du cinéma*, 7, 49

cameo appearances (Hitchcock's), x, 69, *74*, 74, 76

camera angle diagrams, 20–21, 26, 138, *138–139*, *141*

Canby, Vincent, 76

Carroll, Paul Vincent, 60, 61

CBS, 65–66, 75

Chabrol, Claude, 49, 52, 55, 57, 58

Chandler, Raymond, 80n16 (chap. 2)

Chasen, Dave, 73

*Chicago Tribune*, 82n41

cinema projection, 45

Clift, Montgomery, 50, *50–51*

Club 21, 70, 71

Cole, Nat King, 30

collaboration: in art, x–xi; on *The Birds*, x–xi, 8, 9, 13; in film, 3, 17–18; Hitchcock and, xi, 7, 8–13, 16, 22–23, 25, 27; on *Psycho*, 9, 22

Condivi, Ascanio, x

Conrad, Joseph, 57

"Conversation over a Corpse" (television show), 67

Cook, Eugene, 67

Cooper, Gladys, 32

Corey, Wendell, 30

*Coronet*, ix, 27

costume designs, *12*, 19, 88, *90*, *91*

Cotten, Joseph, 50

Coward, Noel, 55